Devil's Blood

by Charlie McLean

(Co-Author: Sacha Rilke)

A REBELLIOUS ROISTERERS AUTOBIOGRAPHY OF HIS RUMBUSTIOUS ROGUISH ROMP

AND

A C[illegible]

In this rollicking au[illegible]nstantly enticed into a ne[illegible]ded and thrown from one sit[illegible]
Our protagonist dozes his way through life without a care in the world, always accompanied by an insatiable sense of humour and mischief.
From childhood to adulthood, he is building his skills to disrupt, corrupt, and deploy mayhem into fine art.
However, beneath the chaos burns a spark of longing and hope throughout his life.
If only, against all odds, could this coveted spark ignite and shine on his illusive dream.

THE DEVIL'S BLOOD

Chapters

APPENDIX

All of the events in this memoir are true to the best of the author's memory. The views expressed in this memoir are solely those of the author. Some names have been changed in order to protect the privacy of the names that appear in the memoir.

All pictures, photograph's and material that appears in the "Appendix" chapters belong to their rightful owners or are on public domains. Where possible or necessary the sources have benn highlighted.

ISBN 978-1-3999-8856-8

Chapter ONE :

"Be sure the sins of the Father..."

My mother told me that when I was born, the German Luftwaffe was bombing the Glasgow shipyards upon the Clyde. She also told me with great amusement that, as a baby, I was at death's door and was given a blood transfusion. She was convinced until the day she died that they had given me the Devil's Blood. Her family consisted of four girls and three boys, I was the second youngest and the naughtiest, always landing in trouble of some sort or another. Luckily, all the rest were normal. Father was away in the Black Watch in Germany, leaving mother on the poverty line. Most goods at that time were on rations, and coupons were used to get sweets.

There were no obese children then, no TV, and no social media. In those days, the majority of people had large families, which meant you were never short of playmates. We would be out playing all sorts of games from morning until night. Of course we would be off into the hills, into the woods, and surrounding ponds and rivers, but there was also danger all around the area. In those days, Fife was a large coal mining area. The slag after the coal was extracted was dumped around each coal mine, and the combustion from the mini mountains would ignite and burn for 20 years or so. As in the tragic events in Aberafan in Wales, where the colliery spoil tips slid down the mountainside and into a local school, killing 116 children and 28 adults. When the trains were passing through Fife, they would slow down due to the workings underneath in the mines. We would climb onto this bridge, jump onto the trains, and throw as much coal off as possible before they picked up speed. Once, a friend of mine fell under the train and lost his leg. One day, after jumping onto the train, we found a large tarpaulin covering the wagon. So, being curious as to what was underneath, we pulled it back and could not believe our eyes. There were guns, bayonets, etc-, etc-. Of course, we threw lots of these off; and drove the police crazy when they found all of the children running around with .303 rifles and bayonets. It transpired that this shipment was on its way to the scrapyard after the war.

One Guy Fawkes day, my brother James was collecting for his bonfire, but wouldn't let me be part of it. So, a little later, I went to where they were storing everything, and set fire to it. Of course, in a little while, fire engines were speeding down the street, and the sky was red down the road. It turned out that the storage area was a chicken run, and there were outside toilets for the flats at the rear. Everything in that area was destroyed. I was in big trouble, again. Mother showed me no mercy with the boiler stick. I shudder when I look back at some of the antics that we kids got up to. From the fire, the outside toilets were destroyed, including the whole of the chicken run, including the chickens. Another time we've tried to steal some cakes from the back of the bakery, and got chased. I ended up climbing over a three-spike fence. I've slipped, and a spike went straight through my hand; however, that did not deter the teacher from belting me on both hands for my troubles. When I was 11, I moved to a new house in another part of the town,which also meant a new school, St. Columbus High School, having passed my 11+. However, we were then graded like sheep into classes A, B, C, D, and E, with A being the highest. I was put into D, with all of the dopes, and consequently soon made new friends. Like attracts like, and we were all full of devilment. The belt, or the taws, as they called it in Scotland, was still in full swing (please excuse the pun).

It was a Catholic secondary school, and the classes were mixed with children coming from different areas of Fife. The danger around Fife was from these burning coal slag heaps, in fact, one of my school friends had his legs badly burned from treading on these slag heaps. I started school at four and a half years of age, and ran away on the first day. Mother made sure I was there every day from then on. St. Brides was a Catholic school, and on Sundays, I would be dragged to the church. I never made alter boy. My head was always full of nonsense, which hasn't changed much to date, and the dose of the belt was applied daily.

Later on in life, I've met up with a school classmate who became a member of parliament for Falkirk; who put the bill through to abolish the belt in Scotland. He told me he used to think of me getting punished daily when presenting the bill.

On the slag heaps, the kids would find fuses that had not gone off when used to blow out the coal. We would undo the fuse to get the gunpowder, and from that, we would make bombs with which we would blow the fish out of the water or the rivers. Unfortunately, later on, a friend accidentally blew his hand off and had to go around with a hook on his hand for the rest of his life. One of many stories from that period of my life. When I was about five years of age, music came into my life. At school, Miss Mullin played Schubert's "The Trout," and I can remember the words to this day. At home on the radio, I heard many of the great singers of the past, such as Enrico Caruso, Benjamin Gigli, Richard Tauber, and John McCormack, then later Mario Lanza. There was no TV then, but I dreamt I would be able to sing like them. This was the start of my dream, but coming from such an impoverished background, there was little chance of ever fulfilling that dream. Around that time, music could be heard from all different quarters. Men walking home at night from the pub, either singing, whistling or playing mouth organs, creating an amazing atmosphere. As children, walking home after playing all day, a gang of us would always start to sing the popular songs of the time, or war songs, etc. Lily Marlene was a great favourite, and the filthy songs that were around at the time that have stuck with me. Once I found a pound note on my way home from school, and I thought I was rich. Unfortunately, I showed it to my mother, who made me take it to the police station to hand it in. I got it back after six months, as no-one had claimed it. In the face of such honesty, where did I go wrong later on? We used to go to the pit road to catch the miners coming home from their shifts to beg them for their leftover lunch boxes. My headmaster wore a big black cloak, and also had a wooden leg. The kids would sing,

"Mr. Tucker, One, Two, Three! Half a man and half a tree!" On this particular day, several of us decided to walk to the River Forth. In those days, we thought nothing of walking all day to get to the beach. But to get there, we had to get through a graveyard.You could see the Forth railway bridge, there was no road bridge then. So there we were, on the beach, fooling around all day. Eventually, we noticed it was starting to get grey and dark, and the only way to the main road home was back through the graveyard. Of course, being kids, we started to frighten each other, and I spied this concrete bunker with the door hanging loose. I went over to take a closer look, kicked the door, which opened, and I peered in and saw these shelves with boxes on them. At this time, it was unbeknownst to me that I had just stepped into one of the infamous trading grounds of the even more infamous duo of Burke and Hare, whom were in the highly moral trade of digging up bodies for the purpose of making a living through things better left untold. As I pulled one of the boxes that I mentioned, it crashed to the floor with bones inside the box. They were lead-lined. My eyes popped out, and I shouted to my friends that we were going to be rich as the lead in the boxed. A few days later, we returned to investigate further. I then got a wonderful idea! The bones would make an interesting bedmate for one of my sisters! So I went ahead with my evil plan, and all hell was let loose. My mother showed me no mercy again, and she dragged me off to the priest, who gave me a severe telling-off along with a slap 'round the head before sending me to the headmaster for punishment. One of my fellow conspirators was also sent along with me. We knocked on the large mahogany door... No reply. So we tried again, no response, I then tried the door handle, which opened slowly. Before my eyes, he was asleep in his chair with his big black cloak, and lying on the table next to him was his wooden leg. I whispered to my friend that I was going to nick it, and he panicked. I picked it up, and we sneaked back outside, putting his leg in the bin. As you can imagine, big trouble and the belt again.

Two days later, whilst walking along the school corridor, coming towards me was the assistant headmistress. She wore a large wig, and all the kids used to wonder if she was actually bald underneath it. Just as she was about to pass me, I said, "Hello, Miss!". "Don't speak to me boy, you are the devil!",she cried, lifting her hands heavenward. With that sudden movement, she knocked her wig clean off her head. The corridor was busy by now, with lots of kids around. We all stared, and she had not a hair on her head. This was the proof everyone needed. We had gardening lessons, and the garden was just down the road from the school. The teacher was Polish, Mr. Savesky. One lesson, he brought this contraption that he placed in the garden to measure the rainfall. Just before the next garden lesson, my friend and I climbed over the garden fence and both pissed into the rain measurement contraption, but of course it had not rained for a week.

The next lesson, of course it was full-up. The class stood staring down at this thing, and the teacher said, "How can this be? It has not rained for a week!". Of course, I started to laugh, and I was captured. Despite being freezing cold, out came the belt. Six of the best on both hands. Every year the thick ones of the school would go and pick potatoes from the farms around the Fife and Kinross as virtually slave labour, but anything was better than being in a school. We were paid pennies. The farmer would mark out stents (distances) that each one of you would have to pick. Of course, I kept moving the stick next to my friend to make mine much narrower. It meant that the chap next to me would have much more to pick. He would say, "How come you are always finished first?" Evil, but funny.

On the way home, we would sing all these filthy songs, which may be lost forever.

"Mary was a country girl and lived in lovers lane, her father was a dirty man, and she was just the same! Early one morning, a sailor came to stay, and that was the beginning of Mary's misery!

He asked for a candle to show his way to bed, and asked for a pillow to rest his weary head! Mary being a country girl and thought it'd do no harm, she jumped in beside him to keep his belly warm!

Early next morning,the sailor he awoke,and took from his pocket a wallet full of notes! Take this my darling,for the damage I have done, I leave in possession of a daughter or a son!

If it be a daughter, a lady she shall be, if it be a son, send the bastard off the sea! Mary lifted a poker and hit him on the head, take that you dirty bastard for shagging me in bed!

Three months later, her belly began to crack, nine months later out popped Jack! Mary had a baby, she called it little Jim took it to the duck pond to see if it could swim!

It swam to the bottom, it floated to the top. Mary got excited and grabbed it by the cock-tail, ginger ale at one and six a glass, if you don't like it stick it up your arse-no questions tell no lies shut your mouth and you'll catch no flies!"

There were dozens more of these songs by unknown composers; it was certainly an introduction to the vocal side of singing. I don't think the priest would have approved. Potato picking would last a month. One of my friends reminded me about taking the candles from around a coffin lying in the chapel for my gang hut. My brother Willy and I went into a condemned row of houses and pulled the rafters out to build a raft. Unknown to us, there were some people still living there, and the ceiling collapsed down on top of them. We ended up in Dunfermline Sheriff's Court, and received a slap on the wrist. That was my first time in court. Another great hero was Johnny Weissmuller, who played Tarzan in the films. The kids would leave the cinema trying to emulate the "Great Call of the Jungle" (I will tell you later how that nearly cost me my life off of the Spanish coast as I tried to emulate). Near our house, there was a chicken run with many huts. The owner lived two doors away. Running alongside the field where all the huts were was a little stream. Further up, there was a man-made dam made up of coal slag. To let the water go through, there were two large concrete pipes. One day, I decided to block them with two plyboards. Mr. Mullin was feeding his hens when the buildup over a few days caused the dam to burst, and he was up to his waist in water. It was as if the dam busters had dropped bouncing bombs. Well, it washed away the hen huts and all the chickens. I was in trouble again. One day at school, we had a lecture from a white father who was an African missionary. He asked the class if any of us were interested in such a vocation. I put my hand up. The teacher said, "God forbid." I used to wonder what I could have achieved in darkest Africa. They would put out money and feed it into the mouth, which would collect for the starving African babies. But the kids in Scotland were also starving. We still have one of those boxes in the house to this day. A rag and bone man would come around to beg for any old rags, and my young brother Willy once took his trousers off and gave them to him to get a balloon.

I remember the Queen Mother coming to Cowdenbeath to open up a new factory, and of course all of the flags were up. At the same time, the famous film “The Charge of the Light Brigade” was being shown in the cinema, and of course all of the kids needed flags for their makeshift lances. What better than the flags for the Queen's visit? Into the valley of death rode the 600. My brother Willy had the potential to become a professional football player. I had a friend who later became a legend in Scottish football, Jim Baxter, who told me, “Your brother is a great football player.” One day, Willy was swinging from a rope, and I happened to be up the tree with an axe in my hand, and chopped the rope. That was the end of Willy's football career. Another time, we were playing behind some prefabs, digging for gold in this black sludge from the mines. I was digging away when I heard “click.” When I dug around this noise, there was a gold-like bar, which I picked up. I thought I had actually found a gold bar.

I shouted to my mate, “I've found gold!”. “Piss off”. He shouted. “Come and have a look, I said!”. He strolled over, and I showed him. “Good God,” he said, and we began digging again and found a lot more of these bars. The more we dug, the more we found. My friend ran home to tell his father of our great discovery, full of excitement. His father couldn't believe his eyes and went to call the police. When they appeared, they dug down and found more and more bars. It turned out they were brass ingots. And the twist is that the man who lived below in the prefab had been taking them home from work for years. We received an award of five shillings. The man was furious and vowed he would shoot us one day. He was planning to cash these in once he retired; one could say he was really brassed off. Most boys were into bird nesting for the egg collections they had. Of course, we would be away all day searching out the various birds nests, including the swans. A swans egg would be your dinner; it was so big. It was very dangerous trying to get to the jackdaw eggs, as they were so high up on the cliffs.

Some of the lads reckoned that if you could get a jackdaw chick, you could teach it to speak, which reminds me. My friend Frankie, who had a rather bad stammer, had a mimer bird. When Frankie used to sing, the bird would copy him with a stutter. One day, whilst we were out bird-nesting, the gatekeeper stopped us. "Right,you have been out stealing birds eggs, haven't you?" he said. Of course, our pockets are full of them. "No, we haven't," I said. "So let me just check!" So with his heavy hands, he slapped us all over our clothes.

"OK, you can go now," he said as he was smirking. Well, of course, all of the eggs were smashed inside our clothes. A very clever man. He had the last laugh. Playing in the woods full of silver birch trees. One day I was hiding and playing soldiers. There was a grassy circle where I was. Suddenly this little animal appeared, walking past me quite undeterred, and disappeared into the woods. I could only describe it as being identical to a Pekinese, but it was the colour of a red squirrel. When I tried to describe to my friend what I had seen, they replied, taking the piss, "It must have been a haggis!". Twenty years later, I was visiting my brother James in Bournemouth, and my nephew was reading a book on extinct animals, and a page jumped out at me. There was one last seen in Scotland in 1870. Sadly, the book is long gone, but I have often thought of going to the Natural History Museum in London to check it out but never got around to it. My brother Willie has a large picture on his wall in Bournemouth of none other. Wait for it. Yes. Nessie! My mother phoned me and asked, "Have you heard what Willie saw?". "No, Why?" I replied. "He saw the Loch Ness Monster!". "Mother," I replied. "I am telling you!". She was adamant. While visiting Loch Ness with his children, one of them noticed something strange in the Loch. So Willie took a photograph of it and was asked to send it to Inverness to be authenticated. Very intriguing indeed. One day, my friend Rodger and I decided to creep in through the window into the church hall for the goodies to eat and drink.

Rodger decided that he was desperate to go to the toilet and found a top hat, which he decided to shit in. Two weeks later, the school show was being presented. A girl from my class was taking ballet lessons. She came dancing onto the stage, and the hat was passed to her through the curtains. She immediately puts it on her head, and something plonks on her head. Big trouble... Again. On the side of the school dining hall, there was a little metal box on the side of the wall. Being curious. I went to investigate and pulled the handle of the box. It opens up into the chimney.

To my amazement, there were a large number of dinner tickets stuck up the chimney that had been sucked up by the backdraft. I was in business, flogging all the tickets to the kids so that they could redeem the tickets once again for another meal. Around the late 1950s, the music world had changed completely. Bill Haley and the Comets, Elvis Presley, Nat Kind Cole, Buddy Holly, and Cliff Richard the beginnings of the rock'n'roll era. You also had skiffles with Lonnie Donegan, Acker Bilk, Connie Francis, et cetera. We were fortunate as we had a large Palais de Danse, and the young ones would come from all over to come and hear the big bands, Joe Loss, Chris Barber, etc. The various gangs of Teddy boys would break out into fights and scuffles on a regular basis. We would organise coaches and go to different dance halls all over Scotland, such as Perth, Dundee, and Edinburgh, which were very popular. We never had much. So after the weekend, we were all skint. So what pennies we could gather together would allow one of us to pay to gotten into the picture house (cinema). Having got in (having previously picked up a tray of toffee apples from the shop), I would then open the toilet door and let everyone else in. There we were all sitting, enjoying toffee apples, taking up a full row, when the attendant came flying down the aisle. "Okay,where did you all come from?" There are only a few other folds scattered around inside. "We paid at the ticket kiosk," I've said,"No you didn't!" he responded, and threw us all out.

When you visited the various towns to go dancing, you would search out the pub with the best sing-songs in them, and of course you would take your turn to get up and sing! This was extremely popular, and there were actually some great voices among the ordinary people. I was always requested to sing "The Lament of Johnny Thomson," who was the great Celtic goalkeeper, who died as a result of an accidental kick to the head from Sam English, a Glasgow Rangers player. Johnny was a Fife lad from Bowhill. I have a great story later on in the book of the singing days, but sadly, as I'm writing this story, I have just heard of the death of the great Manchester United hero Harry Gregg, the goalkeeper who rescued a number of his colleagues who were trapped on the aircraft of the Munich air disaster.

Chapter ONE :

"Be sure the sins of the Father..."

Appendix ONE

Luftwaffe Aerial Reconnaissance of the Glasgow Shipyard

"Image source : The Glasgow Story Archives"

Black Watch Insignia

"Image source : British National Army Museum"

Fordell Colliery Mining Site in Fife, Scotland

"Image source : Fife Mining Heritage"

Fife Pond

"Image source : Get Outside Ordnance Survey"

Dunfermline Sheriff's Court

"Image source : www.scottishlegal.com"

Aberafan Mining Disaster 21st October 1966

"Image source : British Geological Survey"

A Hunting ground for the infamous duo Burke and Hare

"Image source : Photos of Fife Live Journal"

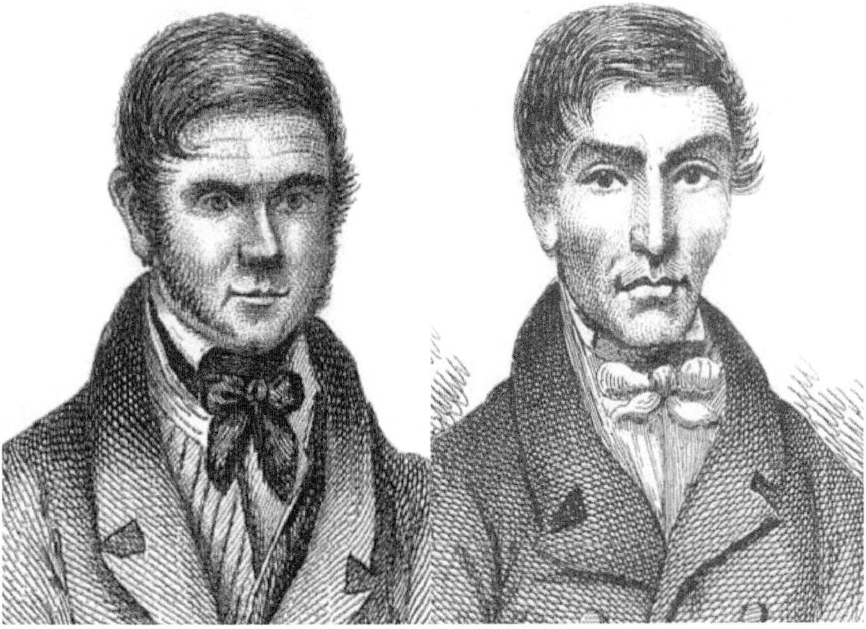

The infamous duo : Burke and Hare

"Image source : Public Domain"

"The Black Baby" Charity Box

"Image source : Private Photo by Charlie McLean"

Painting of the Forth Bridge

"Painted by : Charlie McLean"

IN MEMORIAM

Pictures from : Scottish FA

Poem from : stuartfrew.wordpress.com

Poem written by : Kevin Raymond

"Go on grand-dad tell us,
Tell of us of the day?
When Scotland with Jim Baxter at his best
Beat the England team away"

"Well if memory serves me right
My bonnie wee lad, the story go's like this
Scotland made the trip to Wemberly in '67'
To play the champs of '66""

"Were England unbeatable grand-dad"?
"Unbeatable? Tis hard to say
But Scotland led by Baxter
Sure made them pay that day

With Jules Rimet stood watching
Jim Baxter was our conductor in dark blue
Sent pinpoint passes like greased lightning
Almost thirty, forty yards, it's true

"What did England do grand-dad,
Did they try to stop him playing"?
"Aye my bonnie wee lad, they did try that
But Baxter? He out played them

Grown men were seen to cry the tears
For a nation once more proud
As Baxter and his Scottish peers
Brought cheers that echoed loud

Jim Baxter sat upon the ball
In the middle of the park
Then he'd start the England nightmare off again
With a taunt, a feign, a pass

They tried hard to get the ball off him
My, how those English boys did try
But Baxter tantalized and sucked them in
Then nonchalantly knocked it wide

That game you boys play in the street
Keepie uppie... is it called?
Jim Baxter played that in front of ninety thousand fans,
Right along the Wemberly touchline

The England team were overawed

A young man in his prime he was
Possessed with ball at feet
When England saw him gliding o'er the green
Yon blonde cap'n called "retreat"

Baxter walked about the pitch
A God amongst mere men
He'd beat one man, then turn around
Then beat that man again"

"The scoreline! Tell us granddad
How did it end up"?
"Son, the result? It did nae mean a thing
When you drank the heavenly elixir
From Jim Baxter's dark blue cup

When this game is often talked about
You'll hear praise as old one's sing it
What a match! A terrific victory
But how the hell did Scotland win it?
The other twenty one? Are sadly part of history son
T'was Jim Baxter in a dark blue shirt..... finest ninety minutes"!

"Jim Baxter played in this game as if his very life depended on it"

IN MEMORIAM

"The Lament of Johnny Thomson"
(Unknown)

A young lad named John Thomson,
From the west of Fife he came,
To play for Glasgow Celtic,
And to build himself a name.

On the fifth day of September,
'gainst the Rangers club he played,
From defeat he saved the Celtic,
Ah but what a price he paid.

The ball rolled from the centre,
Young John ran out and dived,
The ball rolled by; young John lay still,
For his club this hero died.

I took a trip to Parkhead,
To the dear old Paradise,
And as the players came out,
Sure the tears fell from my eyes.

For a famous face was missing,
From the green and white brigade,
And they told me Johnny Thomson,
His last game he had played.

Farewell my darling Johnny,
Prince of players we must part,
No more we'll stand and cheer you,
On the slopes of Celtic Park.

Now the fans they all are silent,
As they travel near and far,
No more they'll cheer John Thomson,
Our bright and shining star.

So come all you Glasgow Celtic,
Stand up and play the game,
For between your posts there stands a ghost,
Johnny Thomson is his name.

"They never die who live in the hearts they leave behind."
John Thomson's Epitath

Pictures from theceltiewiki.com

Chapter TWO :

"All in a days work..."

It was not possible to go for an apprenticeship, as my mother could not afford it because my brother James was already an apprentice shipwright at the shipyard in Burnt Island, Fife. As we were surrounded by coal mines, that was it.

"Coal was King!"

So I found a job, not far away at Fordell Colliery, called Alice. Up at 5 a.m. to be at work for 6 a.m. We've first begun at the surface, at the pit head. After a period of time, you would go for training, and eventually, after 16 weeks, you would go underground. The first day I was shown where to go and climb these iron stairs, I could hear the great noise overhead. I opened the door and said to myself, "Help!" To my horror, before my eyes were these moving tables with coal and stones mixed up being shaken along. There were both men and women separating the stones and the coal on either side of the tables, and at the end, the coal would fall down into wagons below,with coal dust billowing everywhere. By the end of the shift, you would resemble a lump of coal, as there were no pit baths then, so you had to walk home as you were. It was only years later that they'd eventually built baths. Winding each other up was a great pastime, and we played lots of tricks on each other, which I haven't grown out of. Young lads came from all over Fife to the training school in Cowdenbeath. After I had finished my training for sixteen weeks, I was eligible to go down into the pit. I had to step into that cage, which dropped down. I suffer from Claustrophobia, so it was like stepping into a dark hell. When we hit the bottom, I asked myself, "What am I doing this for? A few pounds a week?"

The naked lighting on our hats was called carbide lighting, this was the last pit in Scotland to use these lamps. There is a good story to come about those lamps later on.

The monks were the first coal miners, but they got out of their habits quickly (excuse the pun!).

My first job was to control these tubs full of coal, which were ready to be put into the cage to be hoisted up to the surface, emptied, and then sent back down to be refilled. The men would work until they were at least 80 years of age, until they brought in the compulsory retirement age of 65. There were rooms like caves dug out into the walls where you would eat your sandwiches. One of the lads I worked alongside was very cheeky. On one particular day, one of the old boys shouted from next door. "Peter, do me a favour, son?". Peter replied. "Do it your fucking self!". Silence. Five minutes pass, and the old boy shouts again. "Here, Peter... I've got something for you."

So Peter comes out of his cave, into the next door, and up a few steps. He opens the door, and then there is a flash. Peter comes flying out, onto the track outside, holding his jaw. The old man then appears and stands over him. "I bet you're never cheeky again, son!", grinning down at him. How do you live with the shame of being punched by an 80-year-old? Oh, did he get some stick after that. That was the law underground.

Most miners were very learned, they would discuss the arts,music,politics,philosophy,etc. No one ever agreed with anybody else, just for the sake of an argument. From the bottom of the pit, you were sent into the coal face to work with a miner. This was a very old fashioned way of mining.

My task was to push the empty tubs to a miner so he could fill them up. I would then push the tubs to where they would be towed to the pit bottom. This procedure was repeated over and over again until the miner had cleared his quota for the day.

While you were pushing the tubs into the coal face, your face and your back would be hitting against the roof as it was so low. This was a very primitive method of mining. Hessian was used a great deal to divert the airflow into the various sections. As I have already said, the monks were the first coal miners, so one day, an idea came into my head. My evil mind got to work. As ours was a mine where naked lamps were used, I purchased some candles to execute my plan.

Together with two other lads, I began to set it out. With the hessian, we made up some makeshift clothes like monks habits. We set up a table with the candles I had purchased and a set of cards in the section where this particular lad would walk into his place of work the next morning. The plan was set in motion, and this poor, unsuspecting lad made his way into work. He couldn't believe his eyes. He turned on his heels and went running out to the pit bottom, screaming. "There are monks in there playing cards!" Well, he couldn't control his fright. They had to take him up to the pithead to calm him down. Did we get a bollocking for that from the manager? There are always ghost stories circulating in that dark, black world underground. The pit was full of characters. One of my good friends was Jim Baxter, who became the great Scottish football legend. We worked together; he lived at the end of my street and, like myself, loved winding people up. He loved gambling, horses, cards, and tossing the penny (which was a great tradition amongst the coal miners). They would form a circle, tossing pennies into the air and guessing heads or tails.Another character was this little man I worked with; Jockey was his name. He invited me to come shooting with him. I was looking forward to meeting this wonderful dog of his that he was always bragging about. The following Saturday, I met him and set off with him and his arty tweed hat on, with fishing hooks stuck into it, and me looking forward to a duck or a rabbit for tea. A couple of hours later, a rabbit appeared, and he set the wonder dog after it. The dog, a cocker spaniel, goes off into the bush after the rabbit. **Bang! Bang! ...** and the dog is blown away. Well, poor Jockey broke down; his wonder dog was dead. He pleaded with me not to tell anyone. Of course, I couldn't wait to tell everyone. Evil! Of course, later, he swore he would get me in his gunsight one day because of all the piss-taking he had to put up with over that. Some time later, a good friend and colleague of mine, Bertie, had an idea that consisted of us buying a shotgun rifle, as in those days when you turned 18 years old, you could legally own one. The plan was to hunt for small animals like rabbits, hares, or ducks. One day, we've promised my mother that we will go out and hunt for tonight's meal that she would cook. Off we marched, the two of us with a plan in our minds and the rifle in our hands.

Of course, as luck would have it, all day we roamed around in the local forests and ponds of Fife but weren't able to find one single animal that we could have hunted down. The day was coming to a close, and we were equally close to giving up on our idea and our diner. We were walking home on the path that leads to town by the coal mines, where we spotted the pond, which happened to have two white swans swimming gracefully across it. My mind needed no more, and it got to work the usual way. Evil! Before I could have said anything, my friend Bertie was already across and over the fence with the rifle firmly in his hands. It didn't take much conviction for me to follow up. By the time I finally caught up to my friend, he was in position with the rifle shouldered and sighted up, and before I could even say a thing, the familiar sound pierced through my ears. **Bang! Bang!**

The double-barreled shotgun did its job, leaving only smoke coming out of its barrels.

Moments later, I've looked up, only to be greeted by a sight of the two swans, which were not as graceful as they had been just moments ago. It was one thing to shoot them, but now we had another lesser problem that neither of us seemed to have thought of before, which was how on earth we were going to get them out of the water. This proved to be quite a difficult challenge, but we managed to pull one of them out, the other was dragged too far in by the currents and was out of our reach. So here we are, walking and making our way back home to my mother, with the now empty rifle in Bertie's hand and the swan hanging off my left shoulder. Quite a sight we must have been.

After a while, just before sundown, we got home, and as I opened the door, my mother greeted us with an utterly shocked expression on her face. "What is that?!" She asked in shock. "It's a goose!". I've replied with all my confidence at hand. The next morning, me and my brother Willy spent the whole day plucking the "goose" to get it ready for cooking. Some time later, as we were working away, sometimes in silence, sometimes winding each other up, we heard that there was quite a ruckus going on outside and that an army of policemen were rushing down towards the pond by the coal mine, where they had spotted a dead swan floating around. The police were questioning everyone, so we quickly shut the door and hid the half-plucked diner before they'd arrived at us. "You there, son!" shouted one of the constables. "Do you know anything about the bird on the water?". He went on to ask me. "Of course!" I've replied with a quick wit. "The only hunter in town is called Jockey; do you know him perhaps?" I heard a few days later that he'd been arrested. Not long after, I was making plans to get out of the pits with some pals and head to Luton, England. Around this time, JFK became the president of the United States. There was also a local pit disaster at Lindsey Pit in Kelty, where a number of men were killed. Also around this time, Manchester United Football Club sent a football signed by the legendary Duncan Edwards era squad, along with the great manager Matt Busby, who was also from a mining background in Ayrshire, and sent it to the disaster appeal to Russell for those last miners. Shortly afterwards came the great football disaster that ever happened, in Munich,Germany, where most of this great football team was sadly killed. The appeal in Scotland, which had received the signed ball from that wonderful team, sent it back to Manchester.
A true gesture. "The Busby Babes." A very sad period. My dear friend, Jim Baxter, was leaving the pitch because the Raith Rovers had signed him on.

His wages were pennies compared to today's Mickey Mouse players. Jim went on to be a Rangers and Scotland legend. Alex Ferguson commented that "we would not see the likes of his again." I received great honour later in life regarding Jim when he died. Luton was a "boom-town" of that period in 1959. My mother encouraged all the family to move on and travel, most of whom went on the 10£ Emigration Scheme to Australia. The day finally arrived, so with my school friends Tommy McLinden and Billy Copeland, we headed south on the bus and landed in Luton. The digs we found were total shitholes. I found a job in a car factory at Commer Cars Ltd. What a bore that was. I was on the drilling machine all day, boring holes (excuse the pun!). On the move, I later got a job on a night shift in a bakery, greasing bread tins to put bread in on these moving roundabouts. Whilst we were having a break at work, a mate told a story about working summers on the Isle of Wight, working in hotels, on the beach with the deckchairs, and playing football. Plus, all the "birds." My mind was blown-another dream. It sounded like a tropical island. In the meantime, back to greasing the bread tins. This little dictator told me to go faster. As I had just been paid, I picked up this tub of grease and wandered over to where he was working. I poured the tub over his head and walked out the door. I was on my way to the Isle of Wight! (even though I didn't have a clue where it was!) I went back to tell my friends Tommy and Billy about my plans, they said I was crazy, and that it was good there, and I was lucky that I had a good job. Tommy didn't want to go there but ended up as a millionaire, owning a lot of property and an estate on the Isle of Wight. He always was a bit of an entrepreneur. I ended up in Portsmouth, and from there, I took a ferry to the Isle of Wight. I slept that night on the beach. The next day I ended up in Sandown looking for a job, and luck was on my side as I got a job as a hotel porter. I didn't have a clue, to be honest, as I had never been in a hotel. I had plenty of food, a bed, and the money was good – actually much more than I was getting down in the pit, plus the tips.

Two weeks later, my friends Tommy and Billy arrived at the hotel door, and they were starving, so I took them downstairs to the kitchen, where there was this massive pot stewing away on the floor. "Just help yourselves, boys!" I said, and they were like mad men diving into the pot. "This is great!" They've said. I only found out later that that food was actually pigswill. Of course, my evil mind found this extremely funny.

A few days later, a customer requested a pot of tea. I didn't have a clue how to operate this great water geyser, so I asked a fellow worker how to operate it. He was always drinking, and he was a fellow Scotsman from Glasgow. He told me to get out of the way and said, "First of all, you pull this lever,then strike your match." He was demonstrating such a flamboyant, drunken manner. As he put his match to the machine, where the gases had been billowing out for a while, and an almighty **Bang!** and a **Flash!** Filled the room as he was sent flying!

The next day, I saw him looking like a Long John Silver, hobbling down the street on two crutches.

The head porter appeared, and Long John shouted at him (he hated him) and threw his crutch at him. It was hilarious to watch. Each day we would be on the beach swimming, playing football, and general tomfoolery. I thought I had found paradise! We got rid of all the coals from my lungs, and eventually a number of my old friends came down from Scotland, who also found jobs. Of course, it was seasonal work, and you had to plan where you were going to get work for the winter. Sheffield one winter, London the next. My friend Terry said he had been working in a town called Bournemouth for the winter, so off we went. Again, we found hotel work. I later decided to do a government training course in Southampton and then started up again, this time as a carpenter. My brothers Willy and James came back from Australia, and they also settled down in Bournemouth. While working in Bournemouth, I met a blond German girl called Evie at the Westover Road Ice Rink, and before long, I found myself married.

By the time my daughter was born, I had bought a three-bedroom house. In order to earn a bit more income, I had an idea. The area where we lived had a number of foreign language schools, which were always advertising for families to accommodate the students. With this in mind, I thought I would put in a loft conversion. When I mentioned the plan to my wife, she hit the roof. We had a huge row, and she forbade me to go near the loft. Of course, I took no notice whatsoever and immediately sneaked up to the loft to see what I could do with it. In the middle of the loft space was a very large water tank, which held about 70 gallons of water. While inspecting it, I happened to give it a little push, and to my horror, the bottom disintegrated due to rust. "Oh! My God!" There was nothing I could do but shout "Run!" and "Help!" The sheer force of the water blew through the house. There was Evie sitting comfortably on our brand new sofa, knitting away, before the ceiling collapsed, and she was drowning in water and covered in plaster and broken struts of wood. As you can imagine, I had the kitchen sink thrown at me plus a barrage of colourful assortments in English and German. I have to say I found it rather funny with my sense of humour. Some time later, while rummaging in the loft, I came across a painting I had purchased under the influence of a drink. Now a bit more sober, I could make out that it was a copy of the "Mona Lisa," which I felt more appropriately should be hung up in a loo in Bournemouth rather than the Louvre in Paris. I could now see why I paid only £10.00 for it; the eyes were going in different directions. Rather than dispose of it in the skip, I thought I might sell it for a profit. I threw some dust over it and went to phone one of these sharp practicing antique dealers. I told him the picture was covered in dust, but it was of some lady on canvas. Well! He was knocking on the door in no time. He arrived wearing his black Crombie coat and a jewelled pin in his tie. I made out that I was busy downstairs but that he was free to go and have a look on his own. I directed him up the stairs to the loft, where this "masterpiece" lay hidden.

He shot up the loft ladder and, within two minutes, shot down again, crashing down the stairs and nearly tearing the front door off its hinges in his haste to get out. "What a classic!" he repeated over and over again in quite an upset manner, realising that he fell victim to my devilish mind. Building sites were more laid-back than they are now, more like prison camps with security these days. One of the many jobs I worked on was constructing a massive flyover bridge at the rear of the town hall in Bournemouth. Beneath the bridge is a large church, St. Stephens, and we were doing the shuttering and concrete work. One particular morning around 8 a.m. we must have been up at least 70 feet in the air. I was on the edge of the bridge, surrounded by six or seven lads, and I was telling them some sh*t story. Unbeknownst to me, this foreman, George, had been observing me. So over he trots. "Okay, Charlie, I have been watching you for the last half hour, and you have done nothing but talk."

"Fair play," I said "but what were you doing whilst you were watching me?". "Nothing," he replied.

"But I am the foreman." He added. Out of the corner of my eye, down below in the church gardens, was a 15-foot Jesus on the cross. The lads were still around me, and I said, "George, do you see that crucifix down there?" He looks down. "What about it?" he asked. "Well, if you don't fu*k off, there is room on the back of it for you; in fact, I have a hammer and nails handy!" Well, all the boys fell about laughing. A few moments later, George, who was feeling rather humiliated, said, "You're sacked!". That same day, I was walking past the Exeter Hotel, which was being refurbished. I met a lad I knew who asked me what I was up to, and I told him the story of the bridge. When he finished laughing, he told me there were jobs going on in the hotel. So I inquired, was given a job, and started the very next day. Well, the next morning, I could not believe my eyes when I saw what was happening. The lands were helping themselves to all sorts of bedding and furniture as the hotel was doing a complete new refurbishment.

After a few days, I was going up to the main staircase and noticed this massive antique Bavarian-style Coo-Coo clock, which was very old indeed. My mind straight away told me, "That clock is going to be mine!". The cuckoo was more like a golden eagle – it was so big! The next day I was preparing to get it off the wall, and suddenly, without warning, it came crashing down on me, pushing me down the stairs with this giant golden eagle popping out and screaming "Cuckoo!, Cuckoo!" and smashed to pieces! I can't even imagine what it would be worth today if I hadn't done what I did. So, of course, it was time to move on again. A job came up where I will be working all over the country on exhibition work, such as a great show at Earls Court. I also went to Dover to work on the customs shed, where I found fold from back home in Cowdenbeath who owned a pub called the British Queen, and of course I went there because I knew the people very well. Ernest Geraldis and his brothers used to impersonate the famous American group "The Ink Spots." I soon became part of the Dover set. I had permission to employ a couple of labourers. A few weeks went by when I spotted an advert in the local paper for film extras on a movie that was being filmed called "Battle of Britain." Spitfires were flying overhead, and some morning myself and the other folk who had been taken on as extras would meet in the pub for a laugh, and to inspect our RAF uniforms. Not only great fun. They were getting double wages; and none of my bosses came to check what I was up to, so that was great. Eventually, I was given instructions to return to Bournemouth, and that was the end of those jobs. So, as far as I thought at least. I have arrived as per the instructions to the Bournemouth Head Office. I was given the new instructions and information about the next change related to the customs sheds that we were building in Dover. Thus, not too long after, on my way back to Dover with the newfound knowledge that the job is not ending, I passed through the historical town of Hastings, and just as I was reaching the city outskirts, in the corner of my eye,

I noticed a lonely hitchhiker. I stopped and approached the unfamiliar woman to ask which way she was headed, and to my surprise, she was heading in the same direction as mine to Dover to catch the ferry to Calais.

So I told her to have a seat, and I would drive her as far as I could, so she did. After a short amount of conversation, we became quite friendly with each other, so we decided to stop for a coffee before continuing our journey towards Dover. We've spent more time with each other than originally planned, so soon enough I came to the realisation that the sundown is drawing near and the day is coming to a close, so I offered her if she would like to stay with me and spend the night so we can continue on our way the next day.

This plan did not work out the way I had imagined it, and we ended up spending 3 or 4 days with each other at this temporary accommodation, with me sneaking out every now and then to complete my duties and instruct my labourers to carry on with their jobs. My newfound lady companion was adamant that I would join her on her travels, heading towards icy Norway. As I have an easily led nature, I was considering her offer. The next day, my consideration was interrupted by a phone call that came down from Dover.

The voice on the other side of the phone line kept the conversation rather short; it sounded something, or maybe exactly as such, "Charlie, you are sacked!" After these events, I just decided to leave once again, leaving behind a job, labourers, and possibly a broken Nordic heart as well. On top of all of that, I never got my Victoria's Cross for participating in the Battle of Britain. In a few hours time, as I was heading without a real destination towards the south, I'd received another call about a job and a good opportunity in Exeter, near the historical lands of Dartmoor. Without hesitation, I took up the offer, as I felt like I had nothing better to do anyway.

The new job came up, which entailed erecting a small bridge outside Exeter in Devon to accommodate the flood waters that were coming from Dartmoor.

Who happened to be the foreman? You guessed it! George! The very same George who had sacked me after I threatened to nail him to the other side of the crucifix in Bournemouth. There were three of us. One lad from Stirling, Steve, had never worked on a building site in his life, but with my help, he could blag his way through . The other lad was a spitting image of Peter Sutcliffe, the "Yorkshire Ripper." One day we arrived on site, and George saw me. "Charlie!" He shouted, "You of all people!". I told him I had changed. "You better have," he replied. We started the next morning and had to prepare both sides of the bridge for this fairly large stream. Both sides had been dug out, ready for the concrete. If the water got into them, everything would be delayed until the water could be pumped out. I told Steve that if any of the bosses appeared, he should just lift a lump of wood, put it over his shoulders, and walk about as if he were doing something. A few days later, he threw down his long shaft of wood to the ground and told me to f*ck off, saying that he now knew how Jesus felt climbing up the hill with the cross to Calvary and that he must have covered all the stations of the cross. And he meant it. As I mentioned before, if the water got into the holes, nothing could be done until it was pumped out. So when that happened, we would go to Exeter whilst being paid for it. Great! I was actually sabotaging that bank so that the holes would fill up again with water. So we could spend another day in the pubs in Exeter. George was soon on my case, and in front of everyone, he shouted, "Charlie,you are up to your old tricks again!" I know that you are sabotaging the bank and letting the water in." How right he was! "That's it, you are sacked." He shouted. I plaintively told him not to be silly and asked if I would ever do such a thing. "No, that's it," he said. So I set a plan in motion. I instructed "The Ripper," Dave, to nail a couple of railway sleepers together and creep up onto the roof of the office while I would call George out to try and bargain our jobs back. When he came, he'd jump him and nail him to the sleepers, send him down the little river to the sea.

So here I was pleading with George. "No way!" he shouted. Finally, I shouted for him to shake hands and told him we would bid him goodbye. "OK." So out he comes, and this creature, which I can only describe as a double for an orangutan, all 6 feet 4 of him with long, gangly arms and all, leapt from the roof on George. We put him onto the raft made of the sleepers, which we had prepared, and nailed him with his clothes onto it. I told him, "George, you are now heading downstream to the sea," and pushed it into the stream. "Farewell George". He pleaded. "Charlie, you can keep your job." I've replied "George, we're only fooling." I laughed, and we all went up to the pub. George included, and eventually he became a friend. The same night as we were discussing the events of the day, my mind was drawn to an attractive lady, and our eyes had met a few times, thus I decided to approach her. After a rather short conversation, she invited me to her place in Dartmoor. As I mentioned a few paragraphs earlier, when it comes to the ladyship, I am easily led, so no wonder I ended up accepting the invitation, and soon enough, I found myself at her place. A little time passed, and as we were enjoying each other's company, we were suddenly interrupted by the sound of the engine of a large van. "That must be my husband!" She said in a panicked manner, "He'll be just here to pick up his guns!" She added in an even more panicked voice. Without a moment of hesitation or as little as a reply, as I surely did not want to end up the same way as Jockey's dog or the swans on the lake in Fife, I jumped out the window and ran for the woods of Dartmoor at a breakneck speed. A few uneventful days passed by, and as I was thinking about the happenings of the last few busy weeks once again, I received a phone call. What about you, may I ask? A job, surely! This time there was an opening for a position in a cigarette factory that was located in the seafaring town of Bristol. So there I was on my next job, which consisted of putting in a new reception area into a Wills cigarette factory in Bristol. A few days later, I was speaking to one of the security guards, and suggested that there must be a lot of cigarettes stolen from here. "That's for sure, but we can never catch them." He replied. The very next morning, I was taking some of our rubbish, down below to put into the skip when, out of the blue, a body came flying down the shoot! Our eyes met, his face went pink, and behind him, a few big boxes followed. And what was in them, I wondered? Correct! Fags! Well, after a wee bit of blackmail, I was an instant partner. The tune of the day was "I'll Save the Last Waltz for You" by Engelbert Humperdinck, as I waltzed all the way back up the stairs. But you know what? I have never in my life smoked. Why do these situations always seem to follow me? Maybe it's Lucifer guiding me down the path of righteousness. Not long after, perhaps a few weeks, I was back in my home town of Bournemouth and had been receiving strange phone calls. Literally a squeaky voice that was saying, "Mr. McLean, can you come and look at my garden?" I naturally thought it was my brother or one of my mates taking the piss, so my natural reply was "F*ck off!" Anyway, the call continued, so one day I was in the area, and I thought I would check it out. I knocked on the door, and a man opened up. I explained to him about the calls. He told me to come in and took me to Rose, who was in another room. She was sitting up in bed wearing a Victorian bed hat, and I was introduced. "Oh, Mr. McLean," she said, all excited, and started to explain what she would like to have done in the garden. So I agreed to go and have a look around.

Just as I was leaving the room, she called, "Mr. McLean, please do be careful of Bimbo!". Thinking that was a bit of a strange name for a man, I went into the garden and started taking some measurements when suddenly, out of nowhere, near this apple tree, this creature jumped onto my back. I yanked it off immediately, and it ran amok, back up the tree. This was Bimbo! A bloody chimpanzee! So I finished looking around and taking measurements and went back into the house to explain what needed to be done, and she gave me the go-ahead.

Within a few days, I had several men on the job doing different tasks, and Bimbo was happy as Larry up in the tree. A few days went by, and the lady asked to speak with me, so I went inside the house. She was all excited and said, "Oh, Mr. McLean, what a special day it is going to be on Friday!". I hadn't a clue what she was going on about, but she went on. "It's Bimbo's birthday!"
"Oh my God!" She kept muttering.
The next day, I went down to this specialist baker who made one of the wedding cakes for Princess Anne. They specialised in making all kinds of chocolate animals. I asked them if they would consider making a chocolate monkey, but I was told it would be very expensive. Nevertheless, I told him to go ahead. Friday arrived, and I went back to the shop, where they had it all ready in a beautiful six-sided box trimmed with gold and silver and a ribbon in a big bow. It stood about 18 inches high.
I arrived back on the job carrying this box, and all the men asked me what was inside, and I told them not to be so nosey! So I went in the house to show it to Mrs. McVitie and asked her if she remembered what day it was. "Friday!" She replied. "Yes, and what is special about today?" I asked in response, but she had completely forgotten. "It's Bimbo's birthday!", "And what have I got for him?" I showed her the box, and in great excitement, she said, "Oh,let me see!". But I told her it was for Bimbo to open. I told her to sit down, look out of the window, and watch how Bimbo would open it. So I gathered all the men and told them it was a very special day and that I had this big box in my hand, ready to present it to Bimbo. I asked them if they knew what the day was. "Yes, it is Friday," they've replied. I went ahead and told them that it was also Bimbo's birthday today, and what I wanted them to do was to gather around and sing Happy Birthday to Bimbo. As you can imagine, there was a colourful collection of rude remarks. I let them see the lady sitting at the window, and I asked them please to make her day and also Bimbo's, so I kicked off singing a round of "Happy Birthday, Bimbo."

I then told them it was time to play "Ring-a-Ring-a-Roses" and that we must
all fall down holding Bimbo's hand. I don't think there can be many funnier things than seeing the grown men who are also builders carrying out the given task. All big, tough builders! Of course, the little old lady in the window nearly died from excitement, and the box was opened, and there stood this great chocolate monkey wearing a Bimbo T-shirt. The following Monday, I took most of the boys around to the pub, the Pinecliff, and left Peter Morgan to finish breaking up the wall we were building. Peter resembled a Mexican bandit out of a Clint Eastwood movie. We were all sitting in the pub when the door burst open, and there was Peter soaked to the skin. "I don't mind you taking the piss, but when a monkey is laughing at me,that's the ultimate!" We were all in hysterics. We later learned that the monkey had actually lived until the age of 35.

Chapter TWO :

"All in a days work..."

Appendix TWO

"The Alice Pit of the Fordell Colliery

(Location cited as centred on NT 1584 9013). FORDELL

Location: Crossgates

Previous Owners: Earl of Buckinghamshire

Types of Coal: Gas, House and Steam

Sinking/Production Commenced: 1750

Year Closed: 1966

Year Abandoned: 1970

Average Workforce: 509

Peak Workforce: 622

Peak Year: 1959

Shaft/Mine Details: 3 shafts, No. 1 (Alice Pit, NT 1583 9013) 174m, in production by 1894. No. 2 (William Pit, NT 1602 8951) 128m dated from 1843, No. 3 (Lady Anne Pit, NT 1595 8910) 69m deep. Henderson Mine was a drift begun in 1946 and opened in 1948.

Details in 1948: Output 540 tons per day, 145,800 tons per annum. 464 employees. Snack canteen, first-aid room, electricity bought from former Fife Electric Power Company, some steam also used. Report dated 11-08-1948.

Other Details: Situated on the edge of the Cowdenbeath coalfield, and associated with Sir Robert Henderson's wooden wagonway to St David's Harbour, one of the earliest railways in Scotland.

This is the Lady Alice, one of the Fordell Collieries. [illegible]

[illegible]

"Image source : Fife Mining Heritage Society"
"Text source : National Record of the Historic Environment"

IN MEMORIAM

"The Busby Babes"

✞Gone but not forgotten.✞

In memory of the Legendary Manchester United Football team "The Busby Babes"

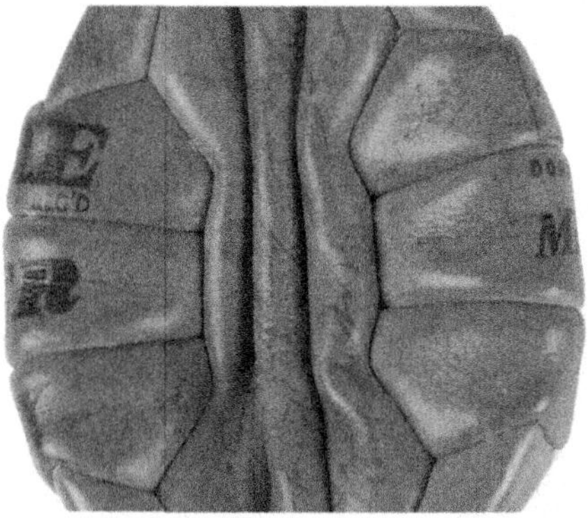

The "Busby Babes Ball"

The ball was signed by Sir Matt Busby, Johnny Berry, Jackie Blanchflower, Joe Carolan, Bobby Charlton, Jack Crompton, Ian Greaves, Noel McFarlane, Albert Scanlon who all survived Munich. The names of Geoff Bent, Roger Byrne, Duncan Edwards, Mark Jones, David Pegg, Tommy Taylor and Liam Whelan, who all died in the disaster, are on the ball with the only absentee being Eddie Colman, who also died.

The Munich Disaster

The team plane made a refuelling stop at at a snow-covered and freezing Munich Airport.

While attempting to take off, the aircraft crashed on the runway, killing 23 passengers and crew, including eight United players along with journalists and air crew.

"Image source : The Mirror and Getty Images"

"Farewell Fife, Farewell Scotland"

The "Beach Boys of the Isle of Wight"

Top Row from Left to Right : Scott, Patrick, Malcolm, My brother James and Terry

Bottom Row from Left to Right : My brother Willy, Myself Charlie McLean and Billy

Plenty of work, plenty of fun, Plenty of great memories.

"Image source : Personal Photo Album of Charlie McLean"

Traveling across the country

"All in a days work..."

"The massive flyover bridge"
in Bournemouth where George was the
Foreman. (excuse the pun)

"Image source : Alwyn Ladell , Flickr"

The Royal Exeter Hotel in Bournemouth
where the "Coo-Coo Clock" sings no more.

"Image source : The Mirror and Getty Images"

The Bristol Tobacco Factory
"I'll Save the Last Waltz for You"

"Image source : www.tobaccofactory.com"

The Battle of Britain Filmset
(I am still waiting for my Purple Heart)

"Image source : BFI Stills Posters and Designs"

Chapter THREE :

"For Better or for Worse"

I was at home one day when the doorbell rang. I opened the door, and there was this lad I knew from many, many years ago, Antonio, so I told him to come in. I knew him from working in hotels when I first came to Bournemouth. He was Portuguese and told me he had something to show me- it was none other than blank car log books. Well, I knew nothing about cars. He had had them printed in Spain and asked me if I knew anyone who would be interested in them. I told him I'd see what I could do, and after giving me a couple of samples and his telephone number, he left. That was the start of a new adventure. I actually knew a couple of people in the motor trade whom I contacted. They could not believe their eyes when I showed them the quality of these logbooks. They thought they were brilliant and would be easy to clone. All they had to do was supply the cars, change the numbers around, and then sell them on. So meeting Antonio was arranged, and the deal was done. They were so good, they could even sell cars to car dealers all over the country. One car, a yellow Ford Cortina, was sold eight times to different dealers all over the country. They felt the car dealers were a fair game, as they were also crooks so having sold them the car, they would then steal them back off the forecourt to put a different set of numbers on it to sell it again. They always made sure they had a spare set of keys! For devilment, they did this with the Cortina eight times. One order was put in for a four door blue Range Rover that had just come out on the market. This man was a big-time builder and wanted it in the company colours. However, because there were so few on the market, it proved difficult to get a new numberplate to clone it with, and they also had to check that there was no HP on it. Eventually there was a phone call from London to say there was a car that had been taken from a garage forecourt in London with the price plastered across the front windows, and that they now had it in another garage safe in the northern part of London. The next thing was to get a number for the cloning from a similar vehicle. Obviously, there wouldn't be anything around this area, so I had to go up to London.

I went and stood on Westminster Bridge for several hours, hoping to find a suitable number. Eventually, I thought to hell with this; it's a waste of time. So I thought I would go to Parliament to visit a lifelong friend of mine who was an MP, Dennis Cannavan. I asked the porter on the door if I could speak with Dennis. He went in, and after 20 minutes out came Dennis and asked me what I was doing in London. I said "Hello!" followed by a statement that sounded exactly as such: "Just take me down to the bar!" So down we went, and after a couple hours, he told me he had an appointment with an Argentinian journalist. He had been critical of the governor of the Falkland Islands, and there's been a bit of a dispute since he called him an Imperial Clown! Which, of course, was interesting to the journalist. So he showed me out by way of the back door, and we said goodbye and stepped outside. I could not believe my eyes. What was in front of me but blue four-door Range Rover. Just what I was looking for. So I made a note of the number. It proved to be clear, and it all went through perfectly, and the builder got his Range Rover. (Later, there is a great twist to this story when it comes out in the trial at the Old Bailey.) Another order came through for a certain model of Jaguar. My friend in London had a small pick-up truck for breakdowns, a tow truck if you wish. Driving down Holloway Road near the woman's prison, I spied the exact Jaguar they were looking for. My friend reversed his truck and hooked it up with his crane, ready to drive off. All was secure, so we drove a short distance when something caught my eye- some movement in the mirror. I looked around, and my God, it was someone in the Jag waving like mad whilst we were still driving it away..."There is someone in the car," I've said in a calm manner. "Piss off," he answered, as he was quite certain, knowing me, that I was taking the piss. I told him to have a look for himself. "Oh, my God! What shall we do?!" He replied in a shocked manner. My brain got to work the usual way, and I replied in a calm and collected manner, "Don't worry! I know! Pull over!" which he did.

So I jumped out and went to the car, where the occupant was screaming his head off like a pig. "Naughty, naughty" I've said, "were you pissed and sleeping it off in the car?" I asked with a newfound grin on my face. "We thought that we'd wind you up a little." "You know, just for the laughs," I added. He nearly ended up in a lock-up in North London, which was rather funny. There are so many other funny stories I could think of as I'm sitting here writing. When it eventually came to a head and the police were arresting people all over the country, I was also arrested and taken up to Hatfield Police Station, which is like something out of Dickens; it was so ancient. The police had arrested loads of cars from all over and put them in a large area at the rear of the station, and while residing in my cell, I had many visits from the police coming to ask me, "Charlie, could you get me such and such a car?!" Many of them found it absolutely hilarious. We got bailed, and the trial went to the Old Bailey. (Yes, that infamous Old Bailey.) During the course of the trial, it turned out there had been actually two cars with the same registration. One had already been found and people had been arrested, and they thought the second one was a threat to the houses of Parliament, because the member of Parliament, Airey Neave, had recently been blown up by the Irish Republican Army (IRA) whilst driving out of the parliament up the spiral car park ramp. Discovering the second Rover with the same registration within the premises of the Houses of Parliament, the bomb squad from Scotland Yard was about to blow up the second car for safety reasons, fearing that there could have been another bomb in it. They have subsequently changed the law to make it more difficult to commit fraud concerning vehicle logbooks. During the trial, I struck a deal with the lawyers that I would not go to prison if I pleaded guilty. So I went before the judge, and I was sentenced to 20 months. What a carve up! I put in an appeal, which took so long to come through that I was out before it got to the High Court, so they stuck me in Brixton Prison.

Most lads in there learned more about crime than they did before they went in, through meeting all the various criminals, learning their ways, and making new contacts all over the country, like an apprenticeship for crime! "How to become a wiser criminal" From Brixton, I was transferred down to Portland Prison, which is perched on the cliff above Weymouth, Dorset. It is an open prison, so you have much more space to move around and meet fellow inmates. Many of them were in for murder. One of them, in particular, was nicknamed; "Dig-Em-Up Dave," who seemingly dug up a freshly buried body and made pie out of it. I got to know many of these lads. One day I was due for a visit from my mother and sister, Mary. So on this day, they were brought into the visiting room and sat round the table (of course, there were many more tables in this large visiting room). So there we were, chatting away, when fellow prisoners came in for their visits and acknowledged me. My mother's curiosity got the better of her, and she asked me, "What are those men in for?" "Oh, many different types of serious crimes, including murderers such as Dig-Em-Up Dave, for example, who made pies out of somebody. In fact, he is known in jail as the "Pie Man!"

So for devilment, I called a few of them over, and some of them actually gave her a hug after she had tremulously offered her little hand to them. On the next page, I would like to share a poem that was written by a fellow inmate who I was serving time with in Portland Prison.

"Criminalised"

(Tony Edwards)

Has she who holds the scales and sword
Been blinded by the legal horde
In case she should complain?
And did they then blindfold her eyes
So she could not observe their lies,
Nor eye them with disdain?

In the legal Inns of decadence,
Hypocrisy has no defence,
And reputations wilt.
Where gout and arrogance abound,
The cups of port and gin are downed
The tranquillize the guilt.

When penalties are handed down
By those who represent the Crown,
On this they should reflect:
If prison cells do not reform,
But only serve to fuel the storm,
Then justice must object.

When politicians rant and rave
About how children misbehave,
The judges nod and bow,
Like a bunch of spineless Muppets,
Punch and Judy seaside puppets,
All holier then thou.

But when the prison gates unlock,
Society will feel the shock
And crime will escalate,
For in that dark foreboding place,
Resentment breeds and gathers pace
Until it turns to hate.

So lady,please,reclaim your scales
To keep the children out of jails,
To save them from the hate.
And take the blindfold from your eyes
So you can see the vicious lies
Concocted by the State.

On the way out, she cried, "Oh, Mary... Oh, Mary..." What are we doing in here? I knew we should never have come. Imagine him introducing people like that to me." Bless her, but even as I am writing, I am again in fits of laughter at the memory! I used to read letters for some of the illiterate gypsies. A mate of one of the lads I read for, Dave, asked me to tell him a lot of lies about what was going on with his wife outside to wind him up! Of course, I found this idea to be extremely amusing, so it didn't take much to convince me. Several days later, he asked me what I thought would be the best way to escape, as I was on the work team outside. So I gave him a suggested escape route, and three days later I was walking in the yard when I spotted this man on crutches making his way towards me, and I asked him what had happened to him. He replied by shouting at me, "You Dirty So-and-So, I jumped out of the window and fell around 40 feet!" That was the wrong window!" I told him while choking on a laugh, as were all the others who overheard us. On my release, a friend I had been to school with in Scotland was coming down to Cheltenham because the person he worked for was bringing his horse down for the big race. He told me to meet him, as he would have a ticket for me. So I went to this pub, which was packed with Irishmen, but I couldn't find them. However, I happened to glance down at what was on the floor a ticket. I couldn't believe my eyes. I picked it up and discovered it was not just any old ticket but a press ticket! I waited and waited but still couldn't find my mates. The next day, I went to the stadium, and as I still couldn't find the boys, I put on the press badge that I had found. Of course, with that, there was no problem getting into the large stadium, through the entrance, and making my way to the press area, I found that the race had already begun. Everybody would rush out to the balconies to watch, while leaving the champagne and fancy food on the unattended tables. So having not been long out of prison, I was obviously rather poor, so I filled myself up from the bounty of the table!

I eventually found my friends who were curious as to how I managed to get in, what was I doing with a load of bottles of drink in my arms, and how I could possibly afford it. One of them I was with had his own horse down for the race and was obviously very proud of it, and he kept asking me what I thought about the horse. I told him with a grin on my face that I known a buyer in France who would be potentially interested in purchasing the horse from him, and his eyes lit up only to be lit down as I continued by stating that the Frenchman buys horses for horse steaks. He left without a word, huffing and puffing. Talking of horse meat, I was once asked if I knew how to acquire it, and I replied that I knew exactly where to get plenty. "Okay, see what you can do," I was told. A few weeks later, I went down with him to the New Forest, near Beaulieu, to check it out. Just then, a beautiful vintage Rolls-Royce appeared. My companion shouted out in joy to me, "Look there! Look there!". I looked up and recognized the passenger in the car right away; it was none other than Roy Orbison the famous musician. We both went over to have a chat with him. He asked what we were up to, but we obviously could not tell him we were out there to rustle up a few horses to steaks! He told us he was going to open a motor museum in the United States, near Disneyland. Sadly, whilst over here, his family suffered a great tragedy, and on top of that, we never got the horses for the steaks we were after. Around this time, together with my two children and my wife Evie, we have already moved from the house on Brassey Road in Winton to Kings Park by the football ground in Bournemouth. It was a much bigger house and was, in fact, two large flats. One of my great loves was still singing, but my wife was continually telling me to shut up. Mario Lanza was my favourite then. I managed to find my first proper job after release from prison, so off I went again to Fawley Power Station, Leap Beach, near Southampton, where a gas pipeline was being constructed to the Isle of Wight near Cowes. They were digging a huge hole on the beach to enable them to build a platform for a giant winch that would pull the natural gas pipeline from the mainland to the Isle of Wight, so we dug this great hole, and the steel fixings were being prepared along with the steel mesh before concreting. One day I happened to be up on the bank looking out to sea and saw this massive ocean liner coming out of Southampton on its way to go around the Isle , on its way to America. I knew that these great liners (such as the Queen Mary and the United States) had to turn round the corner, creating a huge wave like tsunami from a couple of miles away. I watched it coming in and saw three of the four men down the hole still fixing the steel. I quite sadistically watched while this colossal wave came right over and filled up the hole in seconds. Their heads came bobbing out of the hole, and luckily they were good swimmers. They had no idea where that water had come from. I made a habit out of this and was always keenly waiting for one of the liners to pull out. As I took my position to watch the hole fill up with water, it happened three more times, and my mind found it extremely funny. Many years later, I actually stayed at the Queen Mary, which is now a hotel in Long Beach, California, and I asked what had happened to the United States. I discovered that it was about to be scrapped. I asked him why, and I was told it was for the reason to save the Queen Mary, and yet leave the giant of the sea, the United States, to be left to rot, and he told me they were going to look into a few of them. The very next day, after the job on the Isle of Wight is finished, I get a phone call from one of my brothers, James, and he tells me that his American friend, Raymond, from San Francisco, was coming to England and was due to arrive very soon. He was apparently one of the top gourmet chefs in America, and his catering reputation took him all over the country. I was very interested in meeting this man, and only two weeks later I heard that Raymond had arrived. It was arranged that everybody would meet him in the Kings Head pub in Christchurch, Dorset, the following Friday, including my brothers James and Willy, their families, and many of our friends.There must've been about 20 of us there. As the evening wore on, the flow of drinks began to loosen tongues. "Unfortunately," it's also loosening my devilish mind. I opened my big mouth and put out a challenge to Raymond. I told him the proof of the pudding lay in eating. My brothers were cringing because they knew it was the drink talking. I said, "Tell me, Raymond, if I supply whatever ingredients you ask for, will you cook for us, and we shall have a banquet?". "Okay, it's a deal. Get me some venison!" he replied. I know my brothers were now hiding under the table. The next day, my head eventually cleared, and I began to wonder what I'd gotten myself into, having yet again opened my big mouth.

As it happened that very afternoon, I had an appointment with some lads in Christchurch. I had just parked the car and was beginning to walk across a park to the houses when I saw the lads, having parked their van, actually walking towards me. One of them recognized me and shouted, "Charlie! Would you like to buy some meat? Come and have a look in the van." So he took me to have a look, and I couldn't believe my eyes. It was as if I had won the lottery and my prayers had been answered. There before my disbelieving eyes was the carcass of a frozen deer! So obviously, I made a deal there and then. I took it home in the back of the car and then lugged it upstairs into the bath. I phoned my brother Willie straight away. I rather proudly told him I had the deer Raymond had requested. Of course, he called me a liar and put the phone down. The next morning, Willy was on my doorstep. As he entered and started to come up the stairs, my little daughter was standing at the top. "Where is this deer, Marina?" he mockingly asks her. " Oh, it's in the bath, uncle Willie," she innocently tells him. In disbelief, he goes into the bathroom and finds the frozen deer on its back with its legs sticking in the air! "Oh my God, where the hell did you get that from?" I told him not to be so nosy and asked where Raymond was. So the next day Willie appeared along with Raymond, and between them, with the help of my wife Evie, they planned the meal.

It wasn't just a deer, I had also acquired Grouse pheasant partridge, plus the champagne, brandies , et cetera. It took them several days to prepare the meal, which was so large that twenty people sat down at the table. There was everything. It was fabulous, and Raymond spoke about it for years afterwards upon returning to America. I found out later that it had all come from a country club that had been robbed. At the end of every season, during the winter, we would go anywhere in the UK to find work. On one occasion, a friend mentioned going to work for Black 'n' Decker. The factory was in Greenford, West London, one of my mates father worked there. We found lodgings in Ealing and started to work. The time was soon flying. During this time, there was a thick fog, which they called smog, settling down on London, and you could hardly see in front of yourself. Everything came to a halt – trains, buses – It lasted for 11 days, and when it lifted, there was thick salt on the cars, pavements, and roofs. After that, the laws were changed, and burning coal was banned. I received some news that some of my friends were coming down to London to protest the pit closures in Scotland. I joined in the march through Central London, for which I had taken time from work, to show my solidarity with the miners, as I had been a miner once myself. The march started at King's Cross, and there was a huge turnout. As they marched, they were chanting, "We want work! We want work!" A hour went by, and of course I was getting bored, so I said to George, "Fuck this – let's go for a drink!" So we broke away, George myself and the Union delegates, for the pit that had sent them down. They were the two main official delegates for that coal mine. So we went off into the pub, and after a while, George asked where the brothels were, so I told him about Old Compton Street. Off he went without saying a word. Upon his return, we asked how much it cost him. He told us and said it was also a tip for the maid who was looking after the brothel. So we continued drinking. We all got pissed, and the next thing I knew, I was on the bus back to Scotland! So much for my job.

Obviously, the two delegates had no idea what had actually happened in London and the Parliament regarding the protest; everybody was trying to find out so they could report back to the pit of the result of the actions of the Union. Also about the costs and expenses for the two delegates. Well, at the meeting, while the costs were being read out, it came to George Chapel's expenses, which included the about for the brothel worker and the £2 tip for the maid! Well, it brought the house down. To this day, he thinks it was me who slipped that bit of information into the agenda, so now I was stuck back up in Scotland, thinking that I was probably sacked. I received a phone call from my mate in London who told me to get back down because we were being made redundant and the firm was going to pay us off! So down I went, and sure as hell, it was true. I received 8 weeks of wages and an apology. Having thought I would probably be sacked for going up to Scotland, my prayers were answered, and the summer season was about to begin. Back in my digs, there was a knock on my door. When I opened it, there was Phil, a lifelong friend who had been at school with me. "I heard you came into some money," he said. When I asked him what he was doing, he told me he was going down to Butlins at Bognor Regis. He had worked there before as a camp photographer. So off we went and got rooms at Phil's old digs. The next morning, off we trotted to the camp to inquire as to what jobs were available. Phil had no problem because his photography job was still available. I went into the site office and asked if he had any work, and he said there was only a vacancy for a gardener. I replied, "How lucky I am a gardener!" with an enthusiastic voice and the usual grin on my face. "Do you have any proper experience?" He asked. "Oh, yes, of course I've worked at Kew Gardens." I replied. "That's good enough for me; when can you start?". Obviously, I knew nothing at all about gardening. The last gardening I did was when I was a kid and pissed in the weather measuring pot for rainfall back in school in Fife. I thought to myself, "If he'd offered me a job as an astronaut, I would've told him I'd already been to the moon and back, twice, actually." On Monday. I reported to the foreman – this big old boy called Jimmy – who gave me various jobs. Of course, it was not long before the tomfoolery began. The old boy gave me these roses to plant, and I stuck them in!

He went crazy. I innocently told him I genuinely thought that was the correct way, knowing full well that it wasn't. I was pushing the wheelbarrow along when a blackbird appeared. So I put a worm on the end of my boot to see if the blackbird would come and by what means it could get it. In the meantime, I was so preoccupied watching the bird that I didn't notice somebody come up and nicked my barrow. Just then, the foreman appears. "Okay, Charlie, what are you doing?" He asked suspiciously. "I am filling my barrow!" I replied with confidence. "What barrow?" He continued questioning me. "Oh, I didn't even notice! Those bloody black birds will steal anything!" You can imagine the look on his face; it is burned into my retinas to this day. A few days later, I was working with a colleague next to the campus perimeter on a fence. I said he got this idea to put a worm over this little wall and test the people passing by, as we would tell them it was our pet worm and it had escaped. Well, the many different reactions and efforts to get it back to us! From the garden, I went on to be a handyman for the chalets. I soon learnt which ones were occupied and which were empty, and the new business is still being created because I have the keys. A bit of subletting was soon in operation. When I knew one was vacant, we would let it and this became a right little earner. The lads were always looking for somewhere to take their girlfriends. In the camp, there were always singing competitions. I soon got into a few of those, and after one of these events, I was approached and asked to become a Red Coat (The Glamour Boys). Well, that was the ultimate dream job for a young lad. You were like a pop star overnight, and all the young birds were after you. Help! They actually put me in charge of entertaining the children, but I finally got the sack because I was fooling around too much. So back to the Isle of Wight. Phil ended up going back to Weymouth, where he met a girl named Carol, whose father Fred did sand sculptures on the beach by the promenade. The next thing I heard was that Phil himself was now making sand sculptures in Weymouth. Phil was the kind of person who could turn his hand to anything and was always coming up with new ideas. One day he phoned me, all excited to tell me he had just finished a sculpture of Rupert the Bear. These wonderful sculptures were also painted, and the next evening I went down to Weymouth, jumped over the fence, and stole Rupert's trousers! The following day, Phil was on the phone with my brother and was asking him if, by any chance, had I been down to Weymouth recently. When Willie asked him why, Phil said, "Some bastard has been down to Weymouth and stole Rupert the bear's trousers. I'm positive it's Charlie." The next day, he put up a reward for information.

Philip "Phil" Raferty
and
Myself
in Weymouth, Dorset

"Image source : Personal Photo Album of Charlie McLean"

Mark Anderson in the Times Newspaper, he carried on Phil's Art

Image source : "Times Newspaper"

Chapter THREE :

"For Better or for Worse"

Appendix THREE

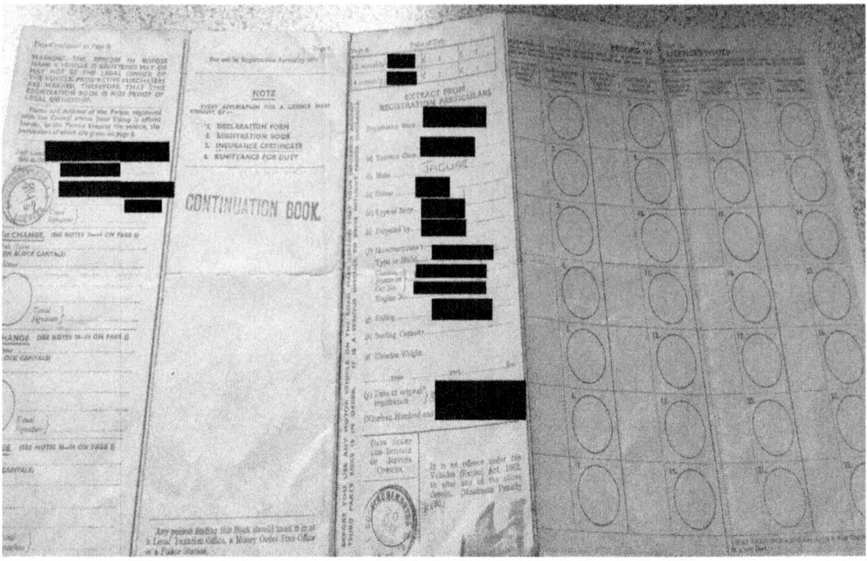

An "Old Green" Logbook and also my first ticket to the building shown below

The cold hospitality of the Dickensesque Police Station in Hatfield

"Image source : Welwyn Hatfield Museum Service"

My first "visit" of many...
Central Criminal Court The Old Bailey

"Image source : Welwyn Hatfield Museum Service"

The Assassination of ✞Airey Neave✞ carried out by the IRA on the 30th March 1979

"Image source : Wikipedia"

My 10 month "Tenancy Agreement" titled "How to become a wiser criminal"
Her Majesty's Prison in Brixton
"Image source : Wikipedia"

"Oh,Mary...Oh,Mary...What are we doing in here?"
Her Majesty's Prison in Portland
"Image source : The Portland History Website"

The construction of Fawley Power Station where they later added the pipelines

"Image source : Powerstations of the UK Website"

Two magnificent vessels, the Titan's of the Ocean at the time

The SS United States Ocean Liner

"Image source : Personal Photo Album of Charlie McLean"

The R.M.S. Queen Mary Ocean Liner

"Image source : Britannica"

Out in solidarity with the miners

Scenes in London's Hyde Park at dinner-time yesterday as the crowds gathered to show their support for the miners. ABOVE: Two historic banners, Upper Clyde Shipbuilders and Albion Motors, the latter with portrait of former Communist shop steward and MP Willie Gallacher. TOP RIGHT: Part of the crowd around the platform. BOTTOM RIGHT: Collecting urgently needed money for the miners. BELOW: The Pit Dragon joins the procession.

Headlines of the Morning Star, previously known as the Daily Worker on the 25th of February 1985

"Image source :Charlie McLean's personal collection of memorabilia"

"...an hour went by, and of course I was getting bored, so I said to George..."

"Image source :Charlie McLean's personal collection of memorabilia"

Advert for Butlin's Holiday Resorts at the time

"Image source : Butlin's Official Website"

"The Self-Catering Flatlets in Butlin's Minehead the ones at Bognor Regis looked similar"

"Image source : Butlin's Official Website"

Chapter FOUR :

“Won't you come home Bill Bailey...”

On a bright sunny afternoon after a long day, we've arranged to meet with a few fellow workmates, Roger and Peter. We were all general builders. There we were, sitting at a corner table in the Pinecliff Pub in Southbourne, Bournemouth. Whilst in there, Roger's brother walked in with another lad who appeared to be more of a gentleman type, wearing sharp clothing, standing tall with a head held high. They've walked over, sat at our table, and joined us for a drink. Through the conversation, it came out that the lad, who was Roger's mate, Alan, was in the carpet trade and had a shop down the road from the pub and a second one down in Parkstone, Poole. As the conversation and the pints kept flowing, Alan revealed that he was actually in big financial trouble. Therefore, he was making plans to leave his sinking ships as the bailiffs were on his tail to take everything he had in order to cover the enormous debt that he had built up over the years.
After a short explanation that lacked the ins and outs or details of depth, he continued by putting it to Roger, Peter, and myself, "Would you like to take over the carpet shop up in Parkstone?". We've looked at each other with the lads, and the general question arose, "What do we know about carpets?" Leaving no time to answer, he continued by mentioning his manager, Roy, who apparently was an expert if it came to carpets and would be able to show us the ropes and quickly get us on track. My mind got to work again in its usual devilish ways as he was mentioning the fact that there was also a flat above the shop that we could use. A decision had to be made quickly. Roger, as it happened, was looking for a flat. The deal was done, and a week later, a meeting was arranged to introduce Roy, and just like that, we all became carpet shop owners in Parkstone. "What a shift in trade!" We met up with Roy, and he agreed to manage the shop. The shop was in a very smart looking parade. Next door was a bank, further up was the post office; it was quite a classy area. The shop was laid out in a first class fashion, with carpet remnants, samples, and displays.

We were meeting with an agent regarding finances to discuss how to move forward. It was quickly stated that credit would not be on offer, as there were large sums owed to most of the carpet companies. With that out of the way, we've opened our doors under the new name "Plush Carpets." Bank accounts, contact books, and all sorts were opened up in a short amount of time, and there we stood with the guys on the day of opening and waited for our first customer to appear. That happened quite quickly, but not in the way we had imagined. A well-dressed man busts the doors open, comes charging in in an obvious state of anger, and straight away goes into demanding his company's carpet samples. Without giving us a chance to reply, he goes on to state that he fully well knows that we are nothing but a front for the previous owner, with to whom he had dealings.

Trying to de-escalate the situation, we allowed him to help himself to whatever belonged to his company. He begins to go through the samples, still obviously quite upset, making all sorts of remarks and comments, one of which was that he would contact all the other carpet companies as to what his suspicions were. After all this, he stormed off, slamming the doors shut behind him. A few hours passed, and we were discussing this matter with Peter, and we decided to phone up the managing director of the company, the "gentleman" who collected the samples worked for. I got onto the managing director and explained what had just happened via one of his agents. I have never been so insulted in all my life. I've added that we've never asked for any credit; we had to pay
pro-forma. We arrived the next morning to find this arrogant salesman waiting for us, samples and all. Plus, eating plenty of humble pie. An offer of credit also! Well, we played around with him whilst he grovelled. He left with his tail between his legs, full of apologies. Much laughter followed him out the door. Roy, our manager, was soon educated about our ways of life. He was the perfect front, ex-RAF blazer, and a perfect gentleman.

Roger moved into the flat above the shop with his partner, Teresa. In life, two's company, and three's a crowd. We soon got the shop moving, and we were still doing our building work, but of course, we never trusted one another.
"Who was fiddling who?" We were soon getting credit again, as we had been paying up front previously. Banks back then were more lenient than today. When a loan came in, it was celebrations down the beaches of Sandbanks. It was the best summer on record. Roy was in charge of the shop, where money was concerned, we would search each other daily. I used to nick the money, take it up to the post office, and send it to myself. Rather amusing. Things have not changed much to this day; true honour amongst thieves, may the best man win.
One day a lady came into the shop, an aristocrat with some sort of a title I forgot by now, but I remember that she was extremely wealthy. At one time, she owned the wool mills in Scotland. She looked around and let us know that she would return tomorrow. In the meantime, Peter meets this waitress from the cafe down the road and invites her back to the shop. He was showing her around the samples, as they'd disappeared and gotten out of my sight. The next thing, this aristocratic lady returns with a friend to show her some samples. I wasn't paying attention. Suddenly, I heard a scream that rang through my ears, and I quickly rushed over and asked, "What happened?!" To my shock, the sight appears in front of me; Peter with this girl from the cafe, literally shagging on the shop floor. I've never seen customers exit a shop so quickly.
One evening, I went to the talk of the town nightclub and was approached as to a deal on carpets. Around 2 A.M. I took this person down to the shop to see what they required. I mentioned to keep the noise down as there is a flat above the shop. Next thing I know, Roger comes flying down the stairs, waving a baseball bat around, thinking the shop was being burgled. "What's going on?!", he yelled. "Oh, just showing a few people around!" I replied. "At this time of the morning?!" He continued on yelling.

I'd been caught red-handed trying to make a deal behind his back. I had the carpet pulled from under my feet. (Excuse the pun.) The next morning; these two ladies came in to complain and wished to speak with the manager.

Roy was on a day off, so I called over Peter, making out that he was the managing director. He appears, with a vest on, heavily tattooed, and two black eyes, as he had been in a scuffle several days previously. Well, it was a sight for sore eyes. With the shock on their faces, they suddenly forgot all their complaints and could not get out of the door fast enough.

Each day, we would plan new ways to promote the business. One day we were offered a van full of electrical goods; we did not ask where they came from (that was never a habit of ours), so with each sale, we would give away an electrical present. Again, this lot disappeared quickly; like I said, no honour amongst thieves. Later on, an invitation arrived from a carpet exhibition at the Metropolitan Hotel in Brighton. So off down to Brighton we went. We were due to arrive there at 10 A.M. we arrived instead at 3 P. M. stinking of booze. One of the managers in there commented, seeing the state we were in, "To think of our trade was to be referred to as the trade of gentlemen," whilst shaking his head. A few uneventful weeks have passed by, and I arrived at Peter's flat, and his wife Barbara opened the door. I hardly stepped in when she kicked off about Peter, who was sitting in the lounge like a little lamb. "Tell Charlie about that slut you have been with!" She hissed at him. "What? My mate Peter? I cannot begin to believe Peter would do such a thing." I said. The drama that had unfolded in the shop previously with the waitress was still fresh in my mind. Well, she never gave up on him. Of course, I was putting my little bit in to keep the fire going. He was trapped, and I was loving it. Finally, she went out and was there, crying with laughter. "Okay, you bastard, have your fun. I swear, I will get you back!" Peter said. Credit at the shop was getting tighter as most of the companies were giving us a wide berth as we were beginning to get behind with our bills.

So I decided to phone up Realton Carpets in Salisbury, they were not too far away. I managed to speak with the managing director and explained what was happening and the accusations made against us by other companies. "Come up and speak to me," was the reply from the other side of the phone line. So the next morning off I went to Salisbury in a large van and met the managing director. Just at that moment, he realised he had an appointment. "Just go in and get what you require; I'll see you on the way out," he said. We loaded the van with all of these large cut-off remnants, and on the way out, I gave him a cheque for £6.500, shook his hand, and wished him all the best. A few hours have passed, and I drove back to our carpet shop, where we unloaded all the carpets I just got. As we were having coffee, three men came bursting in. "OK!" One of them said. "Put all the stuff back." "Pardon?" I said. "Your cheque hasn't been honoured; it has bounced." They argued. "What?!" I said, shocked. "I will sort this out right now!" So I nodded to Peter to go upstairs, and up he went, not knowing what I was planning. I told the men, "I will speak to the bank right away and fix this!" I picked up the phone and put the number in. "Hello, Mr. Cole?" I asked. "Nope," Peter replied. So I had to keep talking as the men were all around me listening. "There are three gentlemen who have come into the shop and let me know that my cheque has not been honoured; it has bounced."

"Are you surprised, mate?" Peter replied. "What should I tell them?" I've continued asking. " Tell them the truth, mate! Tell them that you're a no-good, lying, cheating, conning, devious, slimy bastard!" A lecture followed, "When are you going to go straight in life from your cunning, devious ways?" As promised, he was getting his own back from his other day with the Mrs. I had to keep biting my tongue. He was really putting the boot in. I decided to give the men the phone to speak to the "manager." They declined, thinking everything was sorted out. They left not long after, at which point I went back upstairs to find Peter rolling on the floor laughing.

He certainly had his revenge, saying, "I told you I would get you back one day!" The carpets were soon sold off, and the weather was fabulous, so off to the beach. The next day, during lunchtime, we were returning from the cafe. We suddenly noticed a number of police in the park across from the shop, so we stood back out of sight, watching what was going on.

Suddenly, they all crossed the road, some of them going to the rear of the shop whilst the rest went to the front entrance. An hour passed by, and they all started to leave. It turned out they had a tip off that we were in the process of digging under the floorboards into the bank next door. Roger was due to appear in Bournemouth Court over some affray. As loyal mates we all made our way down to the court to give him support. Well, it went against him, he got 6 months in Dorchester Prison. We were about to leave the court, and I couldn't help it, so I made an insulting remark to the jury, and the next thing I knew, he appeared with two policemen and pointed in our direction. They grabbed Peter and took him away instead of me. He was pleading heavily, but he knew full well that he could not say it was me due to the law of silence and the rules of no grassing. "Look after the shop!" He shouted as he was being dragged away. "Yes mate, just the way you have fiddled me rotten!" I shouted in reply. They held him for most of the night. When morning came, he was being released, and all the way back, he was cursing me with all sorts of remarks, adding, "Thank you for such loyalty!" sarcastically. As we got back to the shop, we wasted no time and placed huge signs outside the shop and on the windows saying, "Grand Clearance!, Everything Must Go!, Closing Down Sale!".

Unbeknownst to us, it happened that the prison van carrying Roger on board was taking the route towards Dorchester via Poole. Unfortunately, en-route, it went straight past the shop. From the tiny window in the prison van, Roger could clearly see the signs in the windows, and he began erratically screaming at the warden, "Stop! Stop the van! My shop is being robbed!" Such was the trust that we had in each other.

As we were sitting down having a coffee with Peter looking at the completed signs, the phone suddenly rang, an old friend of mine, Brian, who was also Scottish. He tells me he wants an extension done and went on to inquire how much would it cost to complete. I told him not much, as I still had a lot of materials that I had been nicking from the sites I'd been working on. He asked whether he would need planning permission, and naturally, I said no. So off we trotted to survey his house. As it happened, his next-door neighbour in the semi-detached, an undertaker,
Mr. Raymond Tombs, who had already had a large extension done that extended the length of his garden. The plan was laid that so Brian's extension work would begin. The next day, while digging out the foundations that backed onto Raymond's extension, the footings gave way and sank down. Raymond's extension served as a Chapel of Rest, and we imagined bodies flying into the hole. Peter went to Raymond to tell him his structure needed underpinning. Raymond gave the go-ahead and the job was completed. When Peter went to Raymond for the money to pay for the work, Raymond refused to pay the full amount. An argument broke out, accompanied by threats, but Raymond didn't budge. Peter's father at the time happened to work across the road from Raymond, in the hospital morgue. A month after the incident, Peter's father called him to tell him he had a friend of his on the slab. "Which friend is that?" Peter asked. "Mr. Raymond Tombs" was the reply, to which Peter reacted by saying
"When you go back to the morgue, give that bastard a punch in the mouth; he still owes me £300 quid!" There was laughter all around. Evil! Not long after the work was completed, I was invited to the boat show in Southampton with my brother Willy. We left in an old van that I had bought from my other brother. I paid him £50 for it. It had Snow Togg written on the side of it for some reason, which escapes me, I was carrying a briefcase, which made me look like an important businessman.

It was around 10 a.m. when we passed an exhibitor selling fine wines, and the salesman collared us. "Please gentlemen! Try This!" and he continued luring us into his tent. I was introduced as Mr. Paisley, and wine tasting and conversation flowed. The salesman asked what I did for a living, and I told him I had a hotel in Bournemouth but unfortunately had left my chequebook at home. He became quite animated by the fact that a hotel was mentioned. We drank the finest samples of French wines and brandies; you name it- we sampled it! We ordered a case load of every single sample we tasted. How we've gotten home, I do not know to this day. The following day, I picked up Peter and his cousin Dennis in the van, which was an absolute wreck. A copper spotted us and pulled us over. "Hello Charlie, What the fuck is that you're in?!" Said the policeman, "I'll only tell you once! Get that fucking heap off the road!" and he added immediately after, "If I see it after today, you're nicked for everything!" and continued by asking, "Is that a fair deal?" I promised to take it to the scrapyard there and then. A mile down the road, an act of God happened. A Fiat came flying out from a side road and smashed into my "pride and joy." My prayers were answered. We all looked at one another. The man was hugely apologetic. Of course I forgave him, as I received £750 from his insurance.

That's the game! Two weeks later, while repairing a sink in a house I was letting to an Iranian couple, a shout came from downstairs interrupting the task; "Mr. Charlie! Mr. Charlie! There is a big wagon outside with goods for you!" I looked out the window and said, "Fuck me!" It was the delivery from the boat show by a French company. "Will you sign for it, Mr. Charlie?" came the same voice. "I'm in the bath!" I shouted. "Sign for me, would you?" Without questioning, he did, and we carried everything in, filling up a whole room with bottles and cases of the finest French booze. It lasted over a year, and "Mr. Paisley" never remembered to pay for it. So anyway, Peter arrives back at the carpet shop the next day with his cousin Dennis.

Without a pause, Dennis goes on to tell us the most amazing story, concerning his mother, Jean. He asked if we could help him. The story was that Jean had gone to the casino at the Royal Bath Hotel and met a man named John Storer and got talking, etc. He tells her he has been through hell, just coming out of a big court case at the Old Bailey for tax evasion. He had been salting money away from the fiddles he was having with his company. The real story ended up coming out a lot later. Dennis asked for help on behalf of his mother. She had married this man; the wedding took place at the Tottenham Hotspurs football ground, as it was a very large wedding. He spent an absolute fortune on her- furs, jewellery, clothes, anything she wished. She was married for two weeks when she decided she wanted more. Storer had a partner in his company that she did not like, and wanted him out. The reason being was that he stood in her way of having complete control over John. That story was put to us by Dennis, and a plan was laid. Jean had asked for help; you could describe her as Joan Collins, a truly beautiful woman. It seems that John Storer had been "loosing heavy machine plant" and claiming it on the insurance, then would resell it in Ireland. The tax man knew nothing about this side of him. His partner was also involved, plus all the other fiddles they were up to. Storer had been telling his new wife everything that they had been up to. The man was besotted with her. She had taken everything she could, it took no time for her to put an evil plan into action. The order was made to make a few phone calls to him. He would either pay up, or we would call the tax man to inform them of his activities. The first call was made from a house in Bournemouth, and the demand was put to him for the sum of £100.000, to be paid. An agreement was reached. A letter with details was requested by John. Over the next few days, phone calls went back and forth. Of course, Jean was at the other end of the phone, seeing his reactions and passing that information back to us. He was prepared to pay up; however the pickup point needed to be decided.

It was arranged that the exchange would take place at Windsor Castle. So we set off: Peter, Dennis, a new face Edward, and myself. The point man would be on a bench just outside the castle gate, where the guard was on duty. I was dropped off on the high street opposite the castle. I had arranged to meet with Storer at a designated spot. I walked around and found the bench, and I could see the guard with his bear skin hat on. I waited a while, then spotted a white Mercedes-Benz drive past. Fifteen minutes later, I saw a man walking towards the bench carrying a briefcase. He sat down. I then approached him. "Excuse me, are you Mr. Storer?" I asked, "Yes," he replied with a rather uncomfortable and shaky voice. "I have a letter for you," I continued. He took it, opened it, and started to read, then opened his briefcase. "Here, take this," he said with shaking nerves. "Are you okay?" I asked. "No, not really," he replied. He bent over and opened the case, which was full of money that was packed in an extremely neat way. I said, "What is this for?" He answered, "You must take it," and continued by stating, "This is the arrangement." I hesitated to take the money. It was sealed in packs of £1,000 bundles. I was carrying a newspaper, and I said, "Put the money in here." I folded the large amount of money in the paper, and he commented that there was more to come. By now, he was really shaking. I suggested that we walk up the road a bit, but by this time, his nerves had really gotten the better of him. I felt something was seriously wrong. From the corner of my eye, I noticed some steps going down into an archway. I felt an overwhelming urge to escape down the steps. I turned to Storer and said, "Okay, I'll see you at the next meet." He looked surprised. And with this concluded, off I went at a quick pace. I had no idea where the archway would lead me, so as I was walking, I was stuffing all the money up my jumper, but there were so many bundles that it made me look like a pregnant duck walking through the empty archway. I didn't bother to look back. Half way down the steps, I heard a number of people following me.

I turned to see three large men following me. I took off without hesitation, running at breakneck speed, holding up my jumper so I wouldn't drop the money. As I began to run, the footsteps of the three large men picked up as well, matching the phase and speed of my own. It was obvious that I was being chased. I arrived at the foot of the steps, where there was a small park, which I crossed and dived over a six-foot wall to make it to an area where there were a lot of turns to get out of the sight of my chasers as much as I could while also hiding the noise of my steps by running on the grass. They did not give up easily, but I managed to build quite some distance up and felt that I was losing them, so I aimed to run towards the pickup point, which was previously decided on. With a great deal of luck, I managed to make it back and jumped into the car where the boys were waiting for me. I just plainly said, while obviously being out of breath, "Get moving!" We sped off; I could hardly catch my breath. "Did you get the money?!" Shouted Dennis. I pulled out the package and showed them all. There were shouts of joy that were not to last for long. When they started opening the newspaper and scrabbled over the bundles, much to their intense disappointment, the contents mainly consisted of mixed paper in between a few real notes on the top and bottom of every single bundle. Dennis went mad, "When you're in a hurry, you don't stop to examine the contents?" I said, being just as mad as he was. "We'll get the bastard for this!" Shouted Dennis, and off we shot to Bournemouth to find out what went wrong. By this time, it was obvious to me that the police were involved. "No ,no! That cannot be." They said. "Yes,Yes! That is the only logical explanation!" I replied. The money I had picked up was shared out as we took the short road home. We continued to discuss who all those involved with the drop-off could have been. Dennis thought they were some of Storer's go–betweens that worked in the tunnels for him; I was adamant it was the police but was outnumbered as both Dennis and Peter agreed with each other.

The next day, the phone was hot in London, where we received an excuse as to why the money had been doctored. My collaborators bought into the explanation, and it was agreed that a meeting would take place at the same location mid-week. Despite much persuasion, I was not up for acting as the pick-up man once more. I told them they were crazy. Instead of me, a new man was picked, Mick Prudd, who had just been released from Dartmoor for his involvement with drugs. He would collect the money. A few days went by when I heard that a police squad from London was raiding our houses. I got on my toes only to find out that Peter, Dennis, Dennis's mother, and Edward had been arrested and taken to London. As a few weeks went by, news trickled through that there had been some treachery and grassing. I went to see a solicitor, who phoned to the police, telling them I would accompany him to the London Police Station. Well! My feet hardly touched the ground upon arriving in London. First of all, I was taken to Cannon Row, then to Stoke Newington Police Station, where Peter, Dennis, and Edward were being held. Then we were all moved around, until finally, we were presented before the **Old Bailey.** We were charged with conspiracy to blackmail. Edward pleaded guilty and was bailed. Peter,Dennis, and by this time Prudd, along with myself, were sent on remand to Brixton with no bail. We went through the booking process at Brixton. Peter and I were sent together, and Dennis, who pretended he was mad, was sent to the hospital wing. Peter and I shared the same cell, a cell for three. As the cell door swung open, there was an Indian man sitting with his head in his hands. He looked up, and I realised he was in a sad, sorry state. We settled in, and I discovered he had been locked up as an illegal immigrant. He asked us what we were "in" for. I nudged Peter with a grin on my face and a shine in my eyes and continued to spin a story about us being body snatchers. Peter straight away picked up on it and continued with more gruesome exploits, such as waiting for funerals, then digging up the bodies and flogging them to hospitals for experiments.

We had the poor bastard out of his head, shaking. The next morning, we were kicked into another cell. This time it was two cells, knocked together. There were three bunks on either side, six of us together, a full house, and a couple of piss pots. Each week, we went to court, but bail was refused every time. Below Peter's bunk was an Arab, who asked me if there were such things as ghosts. I replied, "Are you kidding, mate?!" That started me off. I told him all sorts of stories that had come out of Scotland, and the ghosts I'd seen working down the mines. Just at that moment the screw opened our cell door, popped his head in, and he said, "Just checking the bodies." I looked at him and said, "Excuse me Officer, have you seen any ghosts around lately?" "Ghosts?!" he went on with a shocked expression on his face. "Yes, Ghosts!" I kept going. "You see, when I was in Portland jail, on a few occasions the wind came up and all the doors flew open; another time the prisoners were in their cell when the piss pot in the corner lifted and flew across the cell." I really struggled to keep a serious expression, but I managed, and I could see that the Arabs eyes were bulging out of their sockets as I kept on with my stories. The next day, I had thought out an evil plan in order to keep myself entertained while in this new cell. I acquired a long piece of string and explained to the boys what I had in mind for the Arab. My bed was directly opposite his. Near lights out, I pretended to piss, but tied the string to the handle of the pisspot and made my way back to bed, loosening the string as I went. Everyone pretended to go to sleep, and all was quiet. The Arab's bed was the one closest to the pots.

I started to tighten the string, resulting in a gentle rattle of the pot. The Arab shot up in bed, hitting his head on the bunk above. "Did you hear that noise?!" he nervously asked with a shaking voice. "What noise?" I asked. I repeated the action, which had the same effect every time , and he was told to shut up. I began to pull the pot, and by this time, it was moving past the Arab's eyes. His head went up and he banged against the metal so hard that he nearly passed out.

The pot was still travelling while the Arab was screaming his lungs out, "Ghost! Ghost! God help us! There is a ghost!"
The screws rushed to our cell, and the Arab was dragged away by them to another cell, and I got a beating for my devilment.
In our fifth week "inside," one morning we got a new cellmate. He was below me, sitting on his bunk, writing a letter to his girlfriend. I asked him why he was in prison, and he replied that he had robbed the postman of his bag of mail but didn't get much, only a £4,000 postal order. I said, "I bet you had a good time with that." "Well! He said, I've spent £2,000 and have the other £2,000 stashed away. "Really?" I replied. "You'll never guess where I hid it," he continued. "I was 'round my bird's house when her mother asked me if I would clean out the rabbit hutch." and he continued by explaining that he buried the money under the rabbit hutch. There, as I looked down, was the address on his girlfriend's letter, which I clocked. Peter, who had been all ears, shouted for me to meet him on the prison landing. Peter's first words to me on release were, "Wait for me!" I've said, "What do you mean?" and he continued by saying, "You have that address where the money is." "Peter, my mate," I replied. "Remember how honest you were with me?" He simply retorted by saying, "You cunt!" referring to me. "I will have the limo waiting at the prison gate when you get out, so we can pick up the money together." He knew well what I meant. Two days later, I was given bail. As the prison gate opened, there was my brother's ex-wife. My first words after a quick greeting were "Get me to London!". That was where the rabbit hutch was, but part of my bail conditions was that I was not to go anywhere near London. I was ignored and driven back to Bournemouth. The next day, an old friend from Scotland came to see me. I asked him if he would like to earn some money. I explained what the mission was and told my friend that this chap had asked me to get his money for him and keep it until he came out of the "nick." I continued by explaining that it was in a tin under a rabbit hutch in Basildon, Essex, and that the hutch was at the bottom

of the garden of thereabouts. I advised him to go when it was dark. I also instructed him to phone me at the Duke of Wellington pub should there be any problems. After giving him the telephone number, he set off. I was sitting in the pub when the call for me came in. It was my friend, Phil, who said he could not find the address. I told him to keep looking, and an hour later he rang back to say he had found it, and it was actually quite easy. I told him again to wait until dark. I heard nothing more that night. At 7 A.M. the next morning, my doorbell rang. I looked out of the window, and it was Phil.

"Did you get the money?" I've shouted. "Wait until I come up!" He replied. He sat down to tell me the story. He had crept into the garden when it was dark. He found the rabbit hutch, and laid down, and started to scrape for the tin under the hutch when he saw a man swinging his boot into his ribs. Phil jumped up, startled the man, and they both ran off in different directions. So I said, "You couldn't rob a buck of its doe?" He begged me not to mention it to anyone, but of course I was anxious to tell everybody so we could have a good laugh. Eventually, everyone got bail. We were told it would be a year before the trial. The months went flying by, and our trial was nearing. Five of us pleaded not guilty, while Traynor, who was also one of our collaborators from Scotland, has already pleaded guilty. We had received our depositions from the solicitors, and the truth had started to come out, and it certainly was not looking good. We continued with our normal lives. Still having to report to the police. The severity of the case had not sunken in. All the while, the day to day fiddles continued. A whole year elapsed, and the usual procedures took place. A jury had been appointed and sworn in. The case caught the attention of the media and a few papers, so the gallery was packed to the brim every day. During one sitting, a beautiful girl appeared with jet black hair adorned by a lovely flower. Well! All eyes were instantly directed to the gallery. There was not a head that did not turn- lawyers, barristers, even the judge. She looked as though she had fallen out of heaven.

After a few days, I caught her eye, and a radiant smile came down from above and hit me between the eyes. When I came out of court, there were the usual suspects hanging around, as well as police, lawyers, and barristers, but who should walk out but the Brazilian goddess? I walked straight up to her and asked her to join me for a cup of coffee. You wouldn't believe the looks on those faces watching as we crossed the road to the cafe. The next day, the head of the Serious Crime Squad came across to me, "Charlie!" He said. "I cannot believe you!" and continued by saying, "Here you are, fighting for your life, and there you are pulling a bird. How did you get on with her?" I simply replied with the usual grin on my face, "Don't be so nosey." Well, there she was every day. I never did take up the invitation to Brazil. As the trial went on, it started to look bad for us. The evidence was hugely stacked against us. It suddenly took a turn for the worse when a recording that the police got hold of got played out at full blast in court.

"I will blow your fucking legs off if you don't pay!" I nearly died. I knew nothing of this call being made. One of the co-defendants had already pleaded guilty. In the fifth week of the trial, Mr. Storer was in the dock being questioned as to what he had spent on his new wife, Jean. Out of the blue, Dennis shouts across the courtroom, "I love my dad!"

The reply comes straight away. "I'm not your fucking dad! I only met you once and did not like you then!" shouted Mr. Storer in retaliation. When it came to the officer in charge at Windsor, it turned out that there were over thirty armed police stationed around the castle to apprehend whoever turned up to collect the money that was demanded through blackmail. The judge suddenly broke out in a rage. "I demand to know with that number of officers involved how this man (he's pointing at me furiously) who came to collect the first ransom demand managed to slip through such a highly trained Police Observation Force and escape!"

The officer in charge began to stammer. "I don't want stammering; I want answers! NOW!" The judge kept going on, even more outraged. It transpired that when we left the bench at the meeting, he was supposed to pass me the full briefcase of money. Instead, we left the bench and walked down towards the archway on the other side of the road, much further down the street. Down there, he wrapped the money in a paper bag and said, "You must take this, and I will be in touch." Fortunately, by not giving me the briefcase full of the doctored money. This was the vital mistake in the course of their string. The jury was sent out to decide the verdict. They deliberated for most of the day and finally appeared. The Head Juror was asked the verdict : "Guilty or Not Guilty?"

"Not Guilty," he answered. The judge was even further into his fit of rage, saying that at one time there would never have been a trail for such a case. Celebrations and uproar began.

On her way out of the court, Jean went up to her Majesty the Queen's Council and said, "I want to sue that bastard!" for what he's put me through! This was the first blackmail case to have a Not Guilty verdict at the:

CENTRAL CRIMINAL COURT "THE OLD BAILEY"

Chapter FOUR :

"Won't you come home Bill Bailey"

Appendix FOUR

The former Pinecliff Pub in Bournemouth in a rather unfortunate state

"Image source : Bournemouth Echo (The Lost Pubs of Bournemouth)"

All renewed and preserved! Serving folk once again...What a happy sight!

"Image source : Bournemouth Echo"

"The Carpet Shop"

"It has come to a dead-end"

I find it extremely amusing that it operates as a Funeral Director's these days...
Every time I pass I can still see the signs on the windows stating "The Grand Clearance"
I'm certain Peter would feel the same ... Roger? Maybe not so much.

"Image source : Google Street view Application"

The Royal Stag of Windsor Castle

A rendezvous by the castle followed by a "pleasant" walk that was rudely interrupted by

"Image source : Sunday Times Newspaper"
"Image source : Wikipedia"

CENTRAL CRIMINAL COURT "THE OLD BAILEY"

"The law of the wise is a fountain of life"
"The welfare of the people is supreme"
"Right lives by law and law subsists by power"
"Poise the cause in justice's equal scales"
"Moses gave unto the people the laws of God"
"London shall have all its ancient rights"

"Image source : Assets Londonist Website"
"Image source : Proceedings of the Old Bailey Website"

Appendix FOUR : "Won't you come home Bill Bailey..."

..."Now here is a story of how it begun,
with a phone call from Dennis his dear loving son.
"If you don't pay up you'll go to jail"
the story I'm about to tell you is about the Blackmail."...

"Image source : Charlie McLean's personal music collection"

Chapter FIVE :

"With a Song in my Heart and a Criminal Record"

A few years passed after the trial at the Old Bailey, and I was still up to no good, but that's no surprise. At this time, we had decided with my German wife Evie to go our separate ways, so I moved out of the house by King's Park in Bournemouth to a new one, which was on Valet Close in Christchurch, with my new partner Barbara. This was around the time of the Iranian Revolution, so our town experienced what seemed to be an influx of Iranian nationals who were settling down. The house by King's Park had a good few extra bedrooms, so Evie decided to rent them out to a few newcomers from Iran, whom I later became good friends with. One of them, as time moved on, eventually bought himself a quite large house near Talbot Woods in Bournemouth, which needed quite a bit of renovation before moving in. One day, as I was over, he asked me if I'd be able to erect a perimeter fence around his house, and I agreed to take on the job. Winter was dragging on; it was around February, so the weather was miserable, with a lot of rain and drizzle every day. One morning while digging the fence posts, I had a strange feeling as if somebody was watching me, so I looked around to shake the feeling away, but as I turned, I saw this massive man behind. He must have been around 6 feet 7 inches tall and had a bushy ginger beard. As I turned towards him, he greeted me, "Good morning!" with a deep, gruff voice. "Hello There!" I've replied with a surprised expression on my face. "What are you doing?" He continued. "Well, as you can probably see for yourself, I'm erecting a fence, "I've replied to him. We ended up having a pleasant conversation about mainly construction and the building industry, and at one point during the conversation, I asked him what his type of work was. "I work at Covent Garden," he replied. "Oh, so you are a fruit porter! I see." I went on in a humorous way. "Not quite!" he said and continued by stating, "I'm an opera singer." He continued to tell me all sorts of stories about his line of work as a singer and all the travels and performances that he had.

I just listened and listened as he kept on talking, and when finished, I could only say in reply, "You have made my day!" "Why is that?" he asked. "I've always wanted to be an opera singer; it was a dream that never left me." I replied with excitement. He continued on by asking me if I could sing, and I went on to tell him, the only places I have been singing so far were the pubs back in Scotland, where my audience was mostly either not listening in or completely pissed on booze. "What kind of singer are you?" he inquired. I hadn't a clue, so quite hesitantly, I told him that I didn't know. "Why don't you do something about it?" He continued curiously. "At my age? It's too late for that," I replied with a tone of disappointment in my voice. "You see, I always wanted to sing like the greats such as Caruzo, Gili, Tauber, or Lanza, but I know that at my age that would never happen."As I finished, he looked at me and handed a phone number over while saying, "Call this lady and tell her that I gave you her number; my name is Roderick," and he continued by adding, "I will find out if you have called or not." Later on, I found out that he was the first bass at Covent Gardens. I'm still amazed by how quickly life can turn around and give or take things away without a moment's notice. That early night, as I was making my way back home, I was bursting with excitement and eager to tell Barbara about my encounter. I finally arrived home and began to tell my story to Barbara, and I've added that I intend to phone this number as I'm waving the note that I've received from Roderick. She replied with a lot of disbelief, "Don't be so stupid! At your age?" she continued to put me down. A few days passed and some of my mates from Scotland were having a party, so we were out all night visiting all the pubs that we had fancied, gradually getting more and more drunk as the night went on and the pints flowed endlessly. As the party was coming to an end, the night turned into the early hours of the morning, and I was creeping through my front door, still under the influence of the great atmosphere, conversations, and, of course, the booze.

I stepped through into the living room where Barbara happened to be hoovering, and she looked up at me, and the state I was in, not a word was spoken; instead, she clobbered me over the head with the hoover. *Bang*,*Bang* as loud as Bertie's rifle back in Fife. I guess she took me for a right sucker (excuse the pun). Then she left the room. That evening, as I was sobering up still and the pain was growing from catching the hoover with my jaw, I thought to pluck up the courage to phone the number on the note that had been in my pocket ever since, so that is exactly what I did the coming morning. I woke up and went over the phone and continued dialling the number and as I lifted the phone and listened to the tone, I could feel my throat shrinking due to excitement. Suddenly, a beautiful voice that I could only describe as elegantly angelic speaks out on the other side of the line, "Good morning, this is Anne speaking." I went on to explain what my call was about, but the ladyship did not seem to believe me, I had to describe the man who had given me the number, massive and tall with a big ginger beard and the deepest voice I have ever heard. "Yes, that is him!" After a short pause, which felt like an eternity, the reply came "OK! Come over and bring your music with you." to which I hesitantly replied, "I have no music." The lady told me to go over anyway and gave me her address, and the time to be there. I agreed, and we both said until next time and disconnected the line. Later on in the day, I told Barbara what was to take place and that I had an appointment with a professional opera singer who would be willing to take me on as a student. Naturally, she put me down once again and went on with her speech of discouragement similar to the one a few days ago, such as me being stupid and too old to be doing such stuff and that I should forget about it and should stop being so delusional. Then she left the room. I was sitting there with my thoughts, questioning myself for quite some time, asking if this was really what I should do and that maybe Barbara was right in what she had to say, plus I had this massive pain still growing in my jaw, "I'm just going to make a laughing-stock out of myself if I go over."

After a few hours of self-loathing, I said to myself, "Enough!", This has been my childhood dream ever since growing up in misty Fife in Scotland, to meet and be around people like this and to be able to sing! The appointment was only a couple of days away, so I had to keep repeating the lines above to myself to keep my courage plucked against the panic that was growing as the appointment came nearer by every passing minute. Finally, the day that we discussed with my soon-to-be mentor in the ways of the opera world has arrived, so I gathered myself and what was still left of my courage and made my way to the address that was given. I arrived at the area but was unable to find the exact house at the address, so I searched around in panic, as I was beginning to run late. As the agreed time came by, I was still on my search and was about to give up completely. I started making my way back to where my car was parked nearby, however, my feeling of disappointment was quickly interrupted by the sound of a beautiful melody being played on a piano. I followed the sound through a driveway and a garden, and it led me closer and closer, and as I looked up at the house number, it read out "thirty-two," the same number that was on the handwritten note. "This is it! I've found it." I said to myself in excitement as I approached the window to take a peek. The curtains were slightly open, enabling me to observe what was taking place inside the room. There sat in front of the piano this beautiful, elegant lady, who I thought looked exactly like the famous actress Joanna Lumley, and furthermore her looks matched the voice on the telephone that had been still lingering in my head ever since the conversation. As I was doing my best to take my eyes off the beautiful lady at the piano, a powerful yet subtle voice pierced through my ears as another lady in front of the piano began to go up and down scales, lifting the whole roof with her high notes and placing it back down gently with her low ones.

I was in awe and completely mesmerised by what I was seeing and hearing. I decided to go over to the door and found myself with my finger on the doorbell, but suddenly I was struck by the following question to myself "What have I gotten myself into?" All the courage I was building up suddenly seemed to leave me, and I felt like I was shaking at the knees. My throat completely closed due to panic, and I began to see no other option but to turn my heels and simply flee. During these seconds, which again felt like an eternity, the decision was made for me, as I hadn't realised, due to my panic, that I was actually pressing down on the doorbell. The door to my surprise opened, and there she stood in all her elegant beauty. My new teacher! "Good Afternoon! You must be Charles," she said, and her voice was even finer than it was on the telephone. "Come in, come in," she said, inviting me through this large Edwardian door to her residence. We enter the room, which I was peeking into just moments ago, and she instructs me to take a seat while she finishes the remainder of the lesson with her student present in the room. Here I am, sitting on this comfortable chair in all my discomfort that is lingering still from the days of questioning myself. I'm trying to come up with a plan on how to escape and flee the scene all the while listening to this beautiful soprano being accompanied by Anne on the piano. Anyway, the soprano finishes and thanks Anne for the lesson, and leaves the room. Anne takes a good look at me and sits back down at the piano while instructing me to sing something for her. I can barely muster up words, thus my reply is short "I don't know any of this kind of music," and I continue explaining that I also have a damaged jaw from a recent accident, which later on actually turns out to be cracked. "Oh, I'm sorry to hear about your accident," and she continues curiously, "What happened?". Of course, I couldn't tell her that I was clubbed with a hoover a few days ago, so I just made up a story that went something like falling against the scaffolding on a building site.

"Okay, what we shall do is give you a few simple scale exercises to find out what your range is," she said politely and professionally. I did not know how to do any of the exercises, so she began to show me, and I picked up rather quickly on everything she instructed me to do, so off we went, I'm doing as told and following the piano, doing my best to match the pitch of the notes she plays.

After about 10 minutes, the piano goes quiet only to be swapped with the voice of Anne, who comments with a surprised voice, "You have a very natural and dark baritone voice, but you are able to reach notes above your range, which makes you a rather rare range called a dramatic tenor, and all this with a cracked jaw." There and then we finished the lesson, and she continued by asking me if I would like to return and train my voice with her. Without a moment of hesitation, I replied with an excited "Yes" and after discussing the time and date for the next lesson, we parted.

I couldn't be happier, I was singing all the way home. The next few days were naturally all about me practicing and working on my voice day in and day out accompanied by continuing lessons by Anne, whom we started to become close with as teacher and student. One day, as we were halfway through my lesson for the day, she asked me if I would like to join her and begin rehearsing with her opera group. I was through the roof with excitement and accepted the offer without thinking, and at the end of the lesson, we have discussed the details of the rehearsals. Time seemed to be flying at this point, and I found myself trotting down the road to the Poole Arts Centre to show up for my first rehearsal dressed quite well, as I didn't want to disappoint. I enter through the front entrance and begin explaining to the receptionist why I am there, and she points to the direction of the rehearsal room where I need to go. I had arrived quite early, so at this point, as I entered, I was greeted by an atmosphere that I'd never experienced before. There are singers all over the room.

Some are having a conversation, some are tightening their sheet music stands, and some are going up and down the scales, warming up their voices. Anne quickly recognised my presence, and with a fellow singer on her side, she approached me and introduced me. I went on by explaining to the man in front of me my reasons for being there, and that I barely had any experience, but I was working very hard on my voice under the guidance of my mentor while pointing at Anne standing right next to us. "Ah, yes. I'm quite aware." He replies. "She has definitely heard something in you," he adds in a way that I found quite blunt at the time. As time went on, my life seemed to revolve around everything musical. Practice, practice, and more practice that's followed by lessons, lessons, and more lessons which lead to rehearsals, rehearsals, and more rehearsals. The next thing I knew that there I was singing arias one week in French, another in German followed by Italian, my favourite being the Neopolitans, all of which to this day gives me great pleasure to remember. Naturally, where there are rehearsals, there will be performances and concerts that follow. I performed various concerts with the group all around the south coast of England. Around this period, there were talks in Bournemouth as to closing the well-known and wonderful theatre, the Winter Gardens, which was where the Bournemouth Symphony Orchestra was based at the time, plus all the top stars from all around the world had performed there previously, such as world-famous orchestras or musicians such as Jimi Hendrix, David Bowie, Queen, or The Pink Floyd. The acoustics of the venue were second to none, even the B.B.C. used it for recording. My teacher was approached with the possibility of presenting the second act of Carmen for a project to try to save the Winter Gardens. We all got together to discuss what we could do to participate in the mission to save the venue and were storming out ideas to do so. It took all of us a herculean effort to gather the backing of families and friends of the group, and raising awareness was well underway.

The breakthrough came when we managed to recruit a world-famous and internationally recognised soprano. Now we had a true opera star who agreed that she would become a patron and perform with us. This is how our own company was born, which became the South Coast Opera. The opera was to be led by Patricia Taylor, who was a professional opera singer herself. She studied at the Royal College of Music in Manchester and received the Curtis Gold Medal and the Imperial League of Opera Prize. On top of all this, she won the coveted Richard Tauber Competition, which took her to Vienna and Spain, and she sang with the English National Opera, Scottish Opera, and around the world. She had contacts and wide links with musicians, artists, and operatic performers, so with her on board, we had a really strong team together for the cause, so it didn't take long for us to begin to produce a springboard for the future. Of course, I still had to make a living too, and singing was not putting any bread on my table, so I kept my construction jobs going. I was approached by a friend of mine who was into building new driveways and house fronts with resin-bonded technology, and I decided to create a company with him, and we were making our living out of it. I was never the kind of person who cared much about instructions as such, so I was quite happy not wearing any safety equipment while on the job, which came back to bite me after a few months. I was developing quite a cough, and my chest was feeling quite heavy. I didn't care much for it, as I was certain it would pass soon enough; however, unbeknownst to me, it was the effect of all the toxic fumes that I was breathing in every day while working. Rehearsals became more and more exhausting, and I was left feeling quite breathless at times, but I was sure it was nothing and would soon pass, so I kept pushing and kept my eyes on the dream and the goal with the South Coast Opera. Our newfound opera's first production was Bizet's Carmen, which was to be performed in the Winter Gardens and played for a full house.

I was invited to take on the role of Don Jose, which is a massive part to play. Patricia Taylor would herself play Carmen with the orchestra, so coming from nowhere if it came to the music world, my dream certainly was coming true. The days and weeks were again flying over my head, construction on one side and rehearsals upon rehearsals on the other. I was so caught up in all these new experiences and the hard work that I did not notice that there were a few storm clouds gathering. A growing amount of tension seemed to appear around me within the group; the bluntness of the comment made on the day I first joined as I was being introduced all started to make more sense day after day. I was completely unaware that backstage there were comments and conversations being made about me, and not in a good way. The fact that I was chosen for the role of Don Jose didn't help the growing tensions at all. Even though I had the Devil's Blood in my veins, I was brought up in a way to always encourage anyone, no matter what; hence, I was slow to pick up on the situation. On one particular rehearsal, the other storm cloud was beginning to catch up too, this one being blown over by toxic fumes. I really began to struggle with breathing while performing my part, and I was falling behind. Naturally, for the rest of the group, it didn't take long to notice my voice failing. Eventually, we got through the rehearsal, and it became obvious to me what was going on as many of my fellow performers were making noises and scoffing behind my back. The next rehearsal came, and I had a plan in mind to let them know in a fun and metaphorical way that I was now fully aware of their stance, so before I arrived, I went down to a fancy dress shop, where I found the perfect solution in the form of a sword prop that could be wrapped around my neck and make it seem like I was stabbed through with blood dripping on both sides. I showed up at the rehearsal and approached the particular group that I wanted to send my message to and asked them, "How are you today, boys?" with the sword going through my neck.

They haven't had an ounce of humour so they just stood there. I later found out that they straight away went to Patricia to tell her that my behaviour was frightening. What a bunch of brats, I thought to myself. I found it extremely funny, of course, as I succeeded in winding them up, as I did with so many before them. Unfortunately, this story is only a partial happy ending, as even though the performance in the Winter Gardens was a huge success and, did take place, I had to be replaced as Don Jose due to my rapidly declining health due to all the fumes. However, the success of the performance enabled the Winter Gardens to extend the lease, and the venue survived for a few more years, only to be finally closed down in 2002 and demolished in 2006 to make room for a car park. All this time, we became very close with Anne, and we bonded quite well during all the performances and concerts. My relationship with Barbara, due to the still ongoing and continuous discouragement, was falling apart, so I decided that I would leave her. Shortly after, we parted ways. At this time, it had also become clear that my voice was failing due to the resin fumes, so as I stopped taking on those jobs, my voice began to come back. There were many things to do with the South Coast Opera so naturally, I spent more and more time with Anne, rehearsing, and performing, and after a while, it came that we had grown so close that I decided to move in with her to her large Edwardian home. We ended up getting together and forming a relationship. I started doing jobs around the house, including a beautiful garden and a fish pond in the back. The second largest event that we were running with the South Coast Opera were the Brownsea Island Proms, which were a series of performances all complete with wonderful costumes and sets that had been created by various artists. We have ordered a massive amount of flyers for advertising purposes; in fact, we had so many that we could hardly distribute them, so one day I told Anne that I'd go out and leave them by the doorsteps of the houses in the neighbourhood and the surrounding local area.

Off I went in my usual way, trotting down the road and placing one on every doorstep. The weather was fabulous that day, so there were a lot of people walking by enjoying the usually short-lasting British sunshine. As I was walking past a group of pedestrians, my mind again got to work in its usual devilish ways. I figured that many more people would be able to spot these flyers, but only if I could somehow make them more visible. I was walking past a local hardware store, and the idea shot through my head: "I know!" I said it out loud. I entered the hardware store and went straight up to the clerk manning the cash desk. "Excuse me, sir! Do you sell adhesives?" I said to him: He replied kindly and helpfully and pointed me in the right direction. After a short browse, I paid for my purchase and grabbed my bag, which was full of flyers. I thanked him and left. I headed right back to the busy neighbourhood and got to work sticking the flyers advertising the upcoming event on basically everything I could get my hands on, such as lamp posts, telephone poles, fences, and doors and windows of private houses. It didn't take long, and everything was covered in flyers. When the day came to an end and I was running out of energy and adhesive and my flyers were all gone, I decided to head back home with an enormous amount of excitement to tell Anne how well I had done and that I had distributed all the flyers. She was extremely pleased and happy and asked me curiously, How did I manage to get through such an amount of flyers? I told her that I had a good few tricks up my sleeve with a grin on my face. She replied, "I know, I know. Well done anyway." A few days go by, and I'm reading something on the sofa, and I heard the telephone ring, and Anne is heading out from the other room to answer it. I gave it no more thought. Suddenly, after about 15 minutes, Anne rushes into the room and asks me, "Charlie! How exactly did you distribute all those flyers?" with a panicked voice. I replied by saying, "I made sure that everybody could see them well! Why?"

I am being told that we are going to be fined a large sum of money, as people have called the local council and told them that somebody stuck flyers on their doors and windows. I began to laugh as I found it extremely funny (evil but funny) and told her, "Don't worry, I'll handle it." I went to the kitchen, where there was a local newspaper on the table. I grabbed it and found their phone number, which I dialled. A man picks up the phone and asks me how he can help. I introduced myself as Thomas McLinden, who was a friend who passed away in Fife. I begin explaining to him that I am extremely upset, as I am trying to save our beloved venue with our performances and raise awareness by any means I can, and I get a call from the local council that I have to peel off my ads in order not to get fined. I gave him my contact information, and he told me that they would make sure to put it in the newspaper. That is the story of how I got to the front pages of the newspaper, peeling off flyers with a Union Jack hat on my head. We did not get fined in the end, and my little stunt being in the papers has raised a large amount of awareness. In total, there were three Brownsea Island Proms that we have done, and all of them were massively successful. All this time of performing, rehearsing, and on top of that, still working has definitely depleted my energies, I thought to myself that a little holiday away from England would be due. I knew that travelling around and finding shenanigans would certainly help. I'm sure it was the devil on my shoulder again. I planned a fishing trip to Spain with a friend that would have lasted a few weeks. When I finished planning, I told Anne that I would need a bit of a break, and since there were no further events for a little while, I thought of a fishing trip. When I told her when I would be coming back to England, she reminded me that we were invited to New York by the world-famous soprano, who stood by us in the Winter Gardens performances for her debut at the Metropolitan Opera House. The soprano in question is one of Britain's greatest leading opera singers.

She has performed in virtually every major opera house around the globe, including new productions at Covent Garden, the English National Opera, Paris, Hamburg, Frankfurt, Munich, Berlin, the Vienna State Opera, Athens, The Metropolitan Opera House in New York, San Francisco, Dallas, Houston, San Diego, Carnegie Hall, La Scala Milan, Verona, Florence, La Fenice Opera House, Barcelona, Buenos Aires, and Santiago de Chile. She has performed extensively with all of "The Three Tenors" so it was quite important for us to be there. Anne assured me that I had to be back in time, as the return to England date was just a few days before the travelling to New York. I told her not to worry and began packing. I flew from Heathrow to Malaga to meet my friend, and it was arranged that we would be setting out the following day. We picked up the fishing boat and headed out. It was a Saturday, and the weather was perfect. On a particular day, we had been out at sea for a number of hours when the engine began to stutter and fail. There was black smoke all over and an overwhelming smell of fuel. It turned out that the diesel was dirty, and eventually, the engine died completely, with us bobbing around the Mediterranean, gradually floating in the direction of Morocco during the course of the night. By this time, it was Sunday morning, and as the day got lighter, we spotted a small boat. We signalled like madmen to attract their attention. They eventually spotted us, headed in our direction, and pulled up alongside, tying their boat to ours. As luck would have it, my friend spoke Spanish and was able to explain our situation and that we were stranded. They came on board and tried to help, and as I was observing their boat and its contents from where I stood their cargo, I thought, was not exactly of the legal sort. I turned to my mate and said, "I think they're smugglers." They continued to work on fixing our engine, and I was still looking out to sea when I spotted another boat heading in our direction. It was a much larger vessel, and as it neared, I spotted a large light on its starboard side as well as a gun. I shouted to my mate, "Look what's coming towards us!"

He looked up, as did the Moroccans aboard our boat, who looked extremely concerned. Sure as hell, the boat stopped about 200 feet away or so, and someone leaned over with a long pole and picked something up from out of the sea. It then turned around and headed back to shore. There was neither joy nor success in getting our engine running, so they decided to tow us inshore. The next thing we knew, we were in an inlet, surrounded by mountains on all sides, with spectacular scenery. An hour went by, and another outboard arrived, also full of the same kind of cargo, and in the end, there was a fleet of them. I was getting really fidgety, and as we were surrounded by cliff faces, forming a natural amphitheatre, I had scenes from the movie Tarzan and the voice of Johnny Weissmuller popping in my head. I decided to calm myself down a bit, and of course, to test that wonderful echo, I had the idea that I'm going to perform the famous eight notes of the "Call of The Jungle." So I did. I managed to hit all the right notes and release my powerful roar as loudly as I could. It turned out later that my audience was present, and a few of them decided that I should be thanked by getting my throat cut, as they thought that I was making a signal to the local customs. Our engines turned out to be beyond repair, as they needed a part, and they told us they would take us ashore and put us up in their homes until a part was found. So I jumped onto one of the rubber boats and sat down on top of the cargo, which I was still convinced was illegal, and we rode ashore. From the shore, we drove off into the Atlas Mountains for at least an hour, until we came to a village with a mosque. A few days passed, and I began to panic as I remembered that I was booked to go to New York with Anne, not to mention the fact that all of my clothes, as well as my passport, were

back on the boat. And as I thought it would be a good idea and that it would add to the excitement, I did not apply for a visa before coming to Morocco. I had a long conversation with my mate, and it was decided that in a couple of days, the Moroccans would get my clothes and my passport from the boat and take me to a place where I could fly into Malaga. My mate decided to stay on until they had the required engine part. A couple of days went by, and they came for me. "You!" said one of them in English, "You're on your way!" They got me through customs and into the Spanish Protectorate, where I flew from there to Malaga and from Malaga to London, Heathrow. I knew it was going to be quite tight. Anne, in the meantime, was in complete panic, and feared the worst as I hadn't made it back to Bournemouth yet, but she said to her son, "Oh, he'll probably show up in the last moment with a stupid devilish grin on his face." Of course, she wanted to know where I'd been, and I promised to tell her the story later. It happened as she predicted it would; I arrived at the last minute wearing the mentioned grin on my face. We flew into New York with me being completely unprepared, in summer clothes, and ended up in the Stop the War peace demonstration, which was a strange one. I had to purchase some clothes suitable for the debut. That evening, we fulfilled our goal to attend the Metropolitan Opera House. What a journey! Upon returning to England, Anne and I were invited again by the world-famous soprano to her dress rehearsal of Tosca at the English National Theatre in London. She had sung with Placido Domingo, Jose Carreras, and Luciano Pavarotti. After a few days of rest, we were off to London.

When we arrived and settled at our accommodation, she was going to change into her costumes when she introduced Anne and myself to a lady friend who had her own Shakespearian acting company. I was having a conversation with this lady friend when she told me that her son was a scriptwriter. I had an idea, so I asked, "Would you be so kind as to ask him to ring me?" She agreed, and the conversation came to an end, and we kept mingling. At this time, we were in the middle of planning an event in honour of the famous Scottish poet Robert Burns, which was to take place at the Royal Bath Hotel in Bournemouth. It was to be a large event with a four-course dinner included called the "Robert Burns Supper."

We ended up inviting the world-famous soprano, and she accepted the invitation, which was a great honour, and the event went on to be massively successful. Two weeks later, as I was back home busy in the kitchen, the telephone rang suddenly. I answered it, and there was a man on the other side of the line asking, "Are you Charlie?" with an excited voice. "Who wants to know?" I questioned. The man introduced himself as Jack Jewers, the director and scriptwriter and the son of the lady we've met in London. We began to speak and have a conversation that included a few of my stories, and he got even more excited- so excited in fact, that a few days later after the conversation, he came down to my house to meet in person. We sat in my living room over a few drinks, and he was curiously listening to the stories I was telling him. After a while, he rose up and asked me, "Are these stories really true? Fife and the monks in the mine? The story of the Nordic Hitchhiker, and Bimbo the monkey?" He went on without leaving me enough time to even reply by asking, "Can I return with a fellow writer? This would be an award-winning film!"

We agreed that I would write a manuscript that they could work with, so I began writing, but I was quick to find out that it didn't really give me much fun to sit down and write day after day.

I began to lose interest after a while, and I wasn't making enough progress that could have been worked on so after a while, the project came to a halt. Two years later, I actually received an invitation to the Baftas. Then I called my niece Penny, who now works in Parliament, telling her that I had been invited to London for the Baftas. She laughed and replied, "Are you sure it isn't the daft as Uncle Charlie?" She was so used to my windups and tomfoolery, but went along with it and met me at Waterloo Station, and to her greatest surprise, we actually attended the Baftas in the Strand, where Jack Jewers' short film titled The Storm, which he'd directed, was shown.

A few uneventful weeks have passed by, but it wasn't too long before life got me back into my usual ways. An inquiry came to Anne about whether she could find a star singer to launch Mantovani's new orchestra in America. I heard a sum of £50.000 had been mentioned, and Anne said that she would see what she could do. A few more days passed, and the phone rang. Anne happened to be teaching, so I went ahead and answered it. A deep voice with a broad Yorkshire accent appeared on the other side of the line, asking to speak to Anne. I told him that Anne was busy teaching, and as I said that, my curiosity had gotten the better of me, so I went ahead and explained that was Anne's partner and asked, "Can I perhaps help you?" and continued asking, "What is it you're looking for?" A reply came in a rather sarcastic tone of voice, stating, "An international tenor." I know I use this description a lot, but there is no better one. My mind got to work in its usual devilish ways, so I replied, "Well, you're in luck then!" quite confidently, "What do you mean?" He asked in surprise.

"You are talking to the finest tenor in the world at the moment!" I replied, chuckling to myself. "Can you sing?" he asked. "Can I sing?" I intoned now sarcastically. "Okay, sing me something down the phone." I obliged. "I'd like to meet you in person, Where do you live?" I told him where I lived, and they gave me an address to call in at. I said I'd be there within half an hour and told them to be ready. We hung up the telephone, and I went and entered Anne's studio as she was in the middle of a lesson and began to search through the music cabinet. "What are you looking for?" she asked in a mildly annoyed way. "An old programme, as I have an audition, "I replied while still searching in the cabinet. She looked at the student, who was a bit confused as to what was happening and the sudden interruption, and said, "Take no notice of him."

She thought no more of it, as she was certain that it was just another prank or tomfoolery that I just happened to be up to.

I gathered everything I thought I could need and off I trotted straight to the address that was given to me, and as I arrived to the correct door, he was already waiting for me and had invited me inside. As I entered, I noticed musical instruments neatly organised all around the place, and on the walls there hung large pictures and paintings of the great Montavani. I didn't have too much time to look around any further as he jumped straight behind the piano and requested that I sing. I sang. He then took me into another room and showed me a recording of their first concert. It was fabulous. He asked me whether I could be ready. "No problem!" was my reply, but I had to speak to Anne. I went home with the usual grin on my face and told her that the man wished for her to call him.
"What man?" she asked. I explained everything, and she was in disbelief. She went off to the other room to make a phone call. I tried to eavesdrop on the conversation, but I couldn't hear a thing. Ten minutes later, she came out of the room. "What did he say?" I asked with the grin still on my face, "I'm not telling you!" she said.

A few hours pass by, and there is a loud knock on the door. It's the same man I just had my audition with. We all sat down in the living room, and he began to explain his ideas regarding how to proceed and went into all sorts of details about what must be done. Of course, Anne knew perfectly well that due to the short period of time and the lack of my discipline, it would be an impossible task to prepare me to take on such a massive challenge, so she turned it down and explained to the man that it could not be done. I was quite certain that I could have done it at the time, but now I see that the decision was made for the best interests of everyone, and I already had a good laugh about it anyway. I had been sabotaged! By my own partner!

Chapter FIVE :

"With a song in my Heart and a Criminal Record"

Appendix FIVE

"All images have been taken from the personal memorabilia collection of Charlie McLean"

Courses & Classes

8, SPRING SUMMER 1989

★★

Graham Stockwell

g unaccompanied music
to sight-read music is essential.
ants should contact Mr. G.

Seldown Gallery

TERM:	AUTUMN	SPRING	SUMMER
START:	12 Sept.	9 Jan.	3 Apr.
½ TERM:	–	–	–
END:	–	–	–

Pat Taylor

Dorset Branksea Rooms

– vocal and technical music training, the second – developing
e brought together in preparation for performance.
h March. Fee: $30.

★★

Robin Greenwood

ndividual attention given to
e folk-song accompaniment
les of English, Irish and

Seldown Gallery

TERM:	AUTUMN	SPRING	SUMMER
START:	13 Sept.	3 Jan.	–
½ TERM:	25 Oct.	14 Feb.	–
END:	6 Dec.	14 March	–
SESSIONS:	12	10	–
FEE:	$24	$20	–

★ ★★

rsdays, 7.30pm to 8.30pm

	AUTUMN	SPRING	SUMMER
	15 Sept.	5 Jan.	6 Apr.
M:	27 Oct	16 Feb	–
	8 Dec.	16 March	25 May
ONS:	12	10	8
	$12	$10	$8

Canford Studio
Audrey Archer
Tuesdays, 10.15am to 11.45am

TERM:	AUTUMN	SPRING	SUMMER
START:	13 Sept.	3 Jan.	4 Apr.
½ TERM:	25 Oct.	14 Feb.	–
END:	6 Dec.	14 March	23 May
SESSIONS:	12	10	8
FEE:	$18	$15	$12

g ★ ★★

Canford Room

Rehearsals all set for new opera

Enter, stage right, Poole Opera. The new group is already starting rehearsals as a follow up to an opera workshop group which has already staged local performances.

It is largely the brainchild of husband and wife international singing team Philip O'Reilly and Patricia Taylor. Baritone Philip will be musical director of Poole Opera, Patricia the producer - and they are hoping they don't have quite as many rows as those currently plaguing Paris Opera.

They are joined by Colin Howard who has recently given up his post as head of music at Canford School to concentrate on conducting and is already well known locally as a choral conductor.

Patricia and Philip moved to Parkstone from London four years ago. After the birth of her son, Patricia devoted much time to teaching singing. Her success was such that, for instance, one pupil earned a Royal Opera House contract and others had successful auditions with the Kent and English National companies.

But there are few chances for new singers in established companies, and to give her pupils experience in performance, she presented an evening of operatic excerpts with Chris Dowie, the organist at Wimborne Minster.

This was repeated successfully under the name of the Balmoral Opera Workshop but it became clear something more permanent and ambitious was needed.

Poole Arts Centre were approached and Monday evening rehearsals are getting under way in the Branksea and Dorset Rooms. The idea is not to become another amateur company but to hold courses in all aspects of opera and to pass on experience gained in the professional world of opera. The new group will, however, work towards professionally staged productions with the emphasis on work for soloists and small ensembles.

Those interested can contact Patricia on Parkstone 747398.

THE WINTER GARDENS
THEATRE BOURNEMOUTH
In aid of the Appeal Fund

New Opera's Carmen will aid Winter Gardens campaign

THE newly formed South Coast Opera are adding their weight to the Save the Winter Gardens Campaign with a lavish new production of Bizet's Carmen.

This ambitious show – the company's first major production – will be staged at the threatened theatre at the end of next month.

Although they are also intending to take the show on tour, the company is convinced that the Winter Gardens is one of the few theatres in the region with the necessary stage capacity and accoustic quality to show the production to full effect.

The lead in the show will be played by internationally acclaimed mezzo soprano Patricia Taylor who is also the founder and driving force behind South Coast Opera.

Quality

She originally studied at the Royal Manchester College of Music and received both the Imperial League of Opera Prize and the Curtis Gold Medal.

Patricia made her debut with the English National Opera's production of Menotis Consul. She made numerous recordings as well as radio and TV broadcasts but put her career on hold after the birth of her son.

Now well and truly back in action Patrtricia, who also runs the Ashley School of singing in Lower Parkstone, hopes South Coast Opera and Carmen will put her back on the musical map.

As well as appearing alongside many established local artists, Carmen will also feature a number of performers making their debut in the world of Opera. It opens on September 30 and runs until October 2.

WHAT'S ON

Your daily guide to events in your area

THE Echo's daily What's On listing aims to give you an at-a-glance view of what concerts, plays, shows, films and other events are on in the area.

If you would like your event to appear in this free-of-charge service either write, fax or fill in the form that appears on this page. Unfortunately we cannot accept telephoned information.

Send to: What's On Listings, ... Echo, Richmond Hill, Bournemouth, Dorset BH2 6HH.

TODAY

...ludes regular events.

Tony Reid as Jose and Patricia Taylor in the title role in Opera South's production of Carmen at the Winter Gardens tonight and tomorrow

– Mayfield Gallery, 907, Wimborne Road, Moordown, Bournemouth. Tel (0202) 519044

FAIR – Camelot Craft Fair – Town Hall, Shaftesbury, 10am-4.30pm.

FESTIVAL – Wimborne Arts Festival: ... – The Tivoli, Wimborne.

Road, Bournemouth, 8pm. Tel (0202) 297297.

Opera South presents Carmen by Bizet – Winter Gardens Theatre, Bournemouth, 7.30pm (finishes Sat). Tel (0202) 297297.

TOMORROW

DANCE – Tea Dance, 3-5pm;

author John Hughes, with Mason Gamble as the eponymous hero. Dennis is like a distant cousin of our own Dennis The Menace, if a little more naive. His adventures have a pantomime quality – although older audiences will feel that Walter Matthau steals the show as his grouchy neighbour.

Hot Shots! Part Deux (12) Odeon/UCI

contrast to the dour Henry V, with the only similarity being Branagh's great skill in creating another stylish and enthralling film that speaks to the modern generation as much as the one for which it was written. And we have the pleasure of seeing Denzel Washington, Keanu Reeves and Michael Keaton starring alongside our own Richard Briers and Brian Blessed. Bliss.

Cliffhanger (15) Odeon

That rarest of beasts, the blockbuster that actually delivers what it promises, this is the thriller that returns Sylvester Stallone to pre-eminence in the action genre. Not for the faint hearted though.

Sleepless in Seattle (PG) Odeon/UCI

Old-fashioned, heartwarming romantic tale as two people on opposite sides of America tulfil their destiny and find each other against all the odds. Tom Hanks and Meg Ryan are very believable in their lead roles, while writer/director Nora Ephron injects as much biting wit into the story as she does gentle humour, and has made her best film since When Harry Met Sally as a result.

The Firm (15) MGM/UCI

Strongly adapted from John Grisham's bestseller, Sydney Pollack's fine film stars Tom Cruise as an idealistic young

develops between Ford and his pursuer, wonderfully played by Tommy Lee Jones.

Sliver (18) Odeon/UCI

Would-be erotic thriller, with a turgid, occasionally steamy but more often silly plot and unconvincing performances to match. Sharon Stone is a woman terrorised by a murderer stalking her apartment building; William Baldwin and Tom Berenger are the two prime suspects and prime candidates to share her bed. She deserves everything she gets.

Benny & Joon (12) Poole Arts Centre

Surprisingly mediocre love-against-the-odds comedy drama, starring Johnny Depp – on fine form admittedly – as an eccentric, clownish stranger who falls for the troubled Joon (Mary Stuart Masterson), much to her brother Benny's concern.

Made In America (12) Odeon/UCI/Rex, Wareham

Lame 'comedy' of errors with Whoopi Goldberg as the woman who went to an artificial insemination clinic and thought she was getting the best available – not too tall, smart, black – but realising twenty years later that dumb old Ted Danson was the unwitting donor.

Bambi (U) Odeon/UCI

THE WINTER GARDENS THEATRE
BOURNEMOUTH
Wed. 26th July - Sat. 29th July 1995
PATRICIA TAYLOR
presents
SOUTH COAST OPERA
OPERA GALA
Conductor - KEVIN FIELD
Starring
World Famous Soprano
ROSALIND PLOWRIGHT
£2.50

THE WINTER GARDENS THEATRE
BOURNEMOUTH
Wed. 26th July - Sat. 29th July 1995
PATRICIA TAYLOR
presents
SOUTH COAST OPERA
OPERA GALA
AIDA (Act II)
Madama Butterfly
(Act II)
Boris Godunov
(Act IV)
Full Production Presentation
Starring
World Famous Soprano
ROSALIND PLOWRIGHT
AS AIDA 28 & 29 July only
Conductor - KEVIN FIELD
SHOWS - 7.30pm - SATURDAY MATINEE 2.30pm

rtaincall

Eoin McManus' weekly look at amateur entertainment

inter Gardens for everyone

Taylor sings the title role in
pera production playing tonight
e Winter Gardens

THE Winter Gardens has been saved – and that's very good news.

All those who campaigned long and hard should be congratulated, but let's not delude ourselves in all the euphoria – the tax payers of this town will pay a hefty price to see this concert hall brought up to modern standards.

And not to put too fine a point on it – having paid for it, we had better make sure we use it.

Council leader, Douglas Eyre said he hoped the decision to save the venue would mean people stopped seeing the arts as an "elitist function".

I think that might be a little too much to hope for, but let's hope the powers that be who will eventually control the Winter Gardens aren't too elitist when it comes to letting worthy amateur groups perform there.

Local groups have actively supported the campaign to save the Winter Gardens. They have freely given of their time and talents, and, in the case of The Big Little Theatre Company, actually paid a rental charge for the privilege.

We're told that, under the new scheme, local arts groups will be encouraged to use the facility. This is good news and something which local amateur groups should sieze upon forthwith.

The Winter Gardens deserved to be saved, not just for the sake of the orchestras, which I suspect the threat of losing finally tipped the scales in favour, but for the Bournemouth arts community as a whole – professional AND amateur.

Box Office

Carmen
South Coast Opera,
Winter Gardens
Tonight & tomorrow,
7.30pm
Box Office: 297297

Camelot
Bournemouth
Operatic Society,
Pavilion Theatre
Oct 12-16, 7.30pm,
Mats Wed & Sat,
2.30pm
Box Office: 297297

Whose Life Is It Anyway?
Castle Players,
Lytchett Matravers
Village Hall
Oct 14-16, 7.45pm
Box Office: 623904

Loot
Bournemouth Little
Theatre Club
Oct 18-23, 7.45pm
Box Office: 513361

Iolanthe
Bournemouth G&S,
Poole Arts Centre
Oct 25-30, 7.45pm,
Mats Wed & Sat,
2.30pm
Box Office: [illegible]

WHAT'S ON
The Daily Echo
August 22 1997 7

What's On
Music

TONIGHT:

■ THE PAVILION Theatre, Bournemouth, presents a free lunchtime organ concert at 1.10pm. Tel. 01202 456400.

■ SOUTH Coast Opera and the Dorset Youth Orchestra present a Proms Concert on Brownsea Island today and tomorrow at 7.30. Tickets cost £11.50 and include the boat and admission to the island. £2 concession for families attending matinee at 2.30pm tomorrow. Call Poole Arts Centre on 01202 685222, The Tivoli Theatre, on 848014 or the National Trust on 01985 843601.

Britannia on Brownsea for prom night

Island of opera

Music
by Jeremy Miles

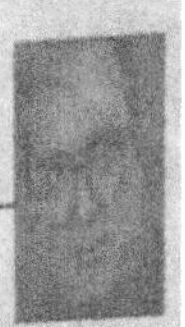

THE innovative and successful South Coast Opera join forces with the award winning Dorset Youth Orchestra tonight and tomorrow to present a traditional and typically rousing Proms-style concert on Brownsea Island.

Featuring South Coast founder Patricia Taylor as principal mezzo-soprano, the show promises to be a block-buster.

A hugely experienced and internationally rated singer, Miss Taylor knows exactly what the real thing feels like, having sung on a number of occasions at the Royal Albert Hall.

The 90-strong Dorset Youth Orchestra, meanwhile, are also a force to be reckoned with. Under the baton of conductor David Norton and appearing for the first time with the SCO chorus, they are likely to produce some extraordinary music.

The orchestra represents the pinnacle of young musical talent in Dorset. Winners of the 1995 Boosey and Hawkes Award 1996, they have just returned from competing for this prestigious award again at the Edinburgh Festival of Youth Orchestras.

The programme consists of the traditional Proms favourites including the *1812 Overture*, the *Carmen Suite*, the *Grand March from Aida*, *Pomp and Circumstance* and the *Chorus of the Hebrew Slaves*.

There will also be a rousing finale of *Land of Hope and Glory*, *Jerusalem* and *Rule Britannia* led by Patricia Taylor. Miss Taylor, founder of SCO, is an international mezzo soprano who has sang many times in the BBC Proms at the Albert Hall.

The concerts come shortly after South Coast Opera received an Arts for Everyone grant in addition to sponsorship for the event from Merck in Poole.

■ Performances are at 7.30pm on Friday and Saturday with a Saturday matinee at 2.30pm (£2 concessions). Tickets, £11.50, from Poole Arts Centre 01202 685222, Tivoli Theatre, 01202 848014, and National Trust 01985 843601

SUPPORTED BY THE NATIONAL LOTTERY THROUGH THE ARTS COUNCIL OF ENGLAND
South Coast Opera
MERCK
PRESENT THE VERY FIRST
Brownsea Island Proms
South Coast Opera
STARRING INTERNATIONAL MEZZO SOPRANO PATRICIA TAYLOR
with the
Dorset Youth Orchestra
CONDUCTOR DAVID NORTON
Fri 22 & Sat 23 August 1997
at 7.30pm 2.30pm Sat matinee
£11.50 PER SEAT
includes return boat fare and admission to Island. Unreserved seating.
AN OPEN AIR EVENT
BOX OFFICE
POOLE ARTS CENTRE
01202 685222
NATIONAL TRUST BOX OFFICE
01985 843601

BOURNEMOUTH Advertiser

Vol III, Issue 275 August 7, 1997 Your priceless weekly newspaper Yelverton Road, Bournemouth BH1 1DD

● Thomas McLinden from South Coast Opera removes one of the posters

Traders are down on the Proms after fly-posting

IT'S A STICK UP!

by Andy Nicholls

THE Bulldog spirit was missing for an opera group when they fell foul of Bournemouth traders and planners.

South Coast Opera, who are staging their own version of 'Last Night of the Proms' on Brownsea Island this month, hit the wrong note by illegally putting up posters to advertise their latest production.

The group incurred the wrath of shopkeepers and Bournemouth council after putting 200 posters on shop windows without the owners' permission.

And the council threatened the group with a £1,000 fine for each poster unless they took them all down in four days.

Red-faced, the group, who blamed an over-zealous member for their predicament, complied with the rules.

Howard Gross, a director of South Coast Opera, said the overenthusiastic member, who he would not name, had been posting posters around Christchurch Road, Westbourne, Southbourne Grove and Charminster Road.

He said the work was carried out in the evenings when the shops were shut and although some shops were empty, the ones which opened next day duly complained.

He told The Advertiser: "I understand the council's attitude. We have taken prompt action to redress the situation."

He said the member did not know the rules about fly-posting and had acted in all innocence. Mr Gross added: "He is very helpful. He just got carried away. He's very embarrassed about it and has promised to clean up his act. We have taken steps so it won't happen again.

"It is a misunderstanding which caused a lot of phone calls from angry landlords, property owners and shop owners. They were upset and having upset them, we are doing our best to put it right."

A Bournemouth council spokesman said all the posters had been taken down: "They had to come down. That is the law. It was all quite amicable."

● Thomas McLinden from South Coast Opera removes one of the posters

Appendix FIVE : "With a song in my Heart and a Criminal Record" 104

The Daily ECHO
WHAT'S ON
TV GUIDE
FRIDAY AUGUST 22 1997
GUIDE TO
THE WEEK'S
SOOTY
comes to
page 2
BANK
HOLIDAY
Show round-up
centre pages
Events listings
starts page 10
FUNNY
MAN
Bradley Walsh
interview
page 24
RULE
BRITANNIA
Proms on Brownsea Island
page 7

Appendix FIVE : "With a song in my Heart and a Criminal Record"

South Coast Opera in the Park

Dates

Sunday	April 7th	Variety
Sunday	May 26th	Variety
Sunday	June 2nd	Variety
Friday	June 7th	Opera Pops
Sunday	June 16th	Variety
Thursday	June 20th	Opera Pops
Sunday	July 14th	Variety
Wednesday	August 7th*	Children
Wednesday	August 21st*	Children
Sunday	Sept 15th	Variety
Sunday	Sept 22nd	End of Season

NB *
The August dates are during the Bournemouth Festival of Lights

Stage Crew

Project Manager - Karen Wells
Producers - Patricia Taylor, Karen Wells
Compere - Andrea Rosenfeld
Accompanists
- Patricia Bonelli, Christine Taylor, Jean Wierzbika
Liaison - Howard Gross
Scenery - Sarah Louise Blake
Sound - David Freeman
Ground Team - Helen Jones
- Plus helpers

BIZET'S
CARMEN
SOUTH COAST OPERA
Beautifully costumed ~ Full orchestral accompaniment
28-29-30 March at 8.00pm
TIVOLI THEATRE
Box office 01202 848014

Appendix FIVE : "With a song in my Heart and a Criminal Record"

South Coast Opera

Presents

A Gala Burns Night

at

The Royal Bath Hotel

on

Friday 20th January 1995

7.30 for 8.00

Dress Formal (Kilts) £28.50

14

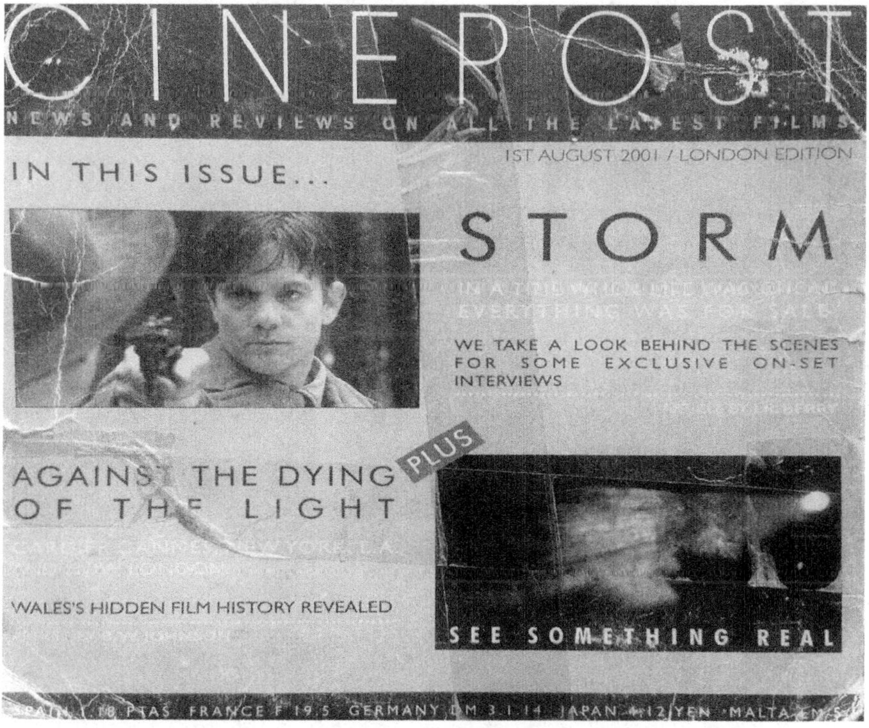

CINEPOST

NEWS AND REVIEWS ON ALL THE LATEST FILMS

1ST AUGUST 2001 / LONDON EDITION

IN THIS ISSUE...

STORM

WE TAKE A LOOK BEHIND THE SCENES FOR SOME EXCLUSIVE ON-SET INTERVIEWS

PLUS

AGAINST THE DYING OF THE LIGHT

WALES'S HIDDEN FILM HISTORY REVEALED

SEE SOMETHING REAL

Chapter SIX :

"The Soul that Sinneth ...it shall Fly"

A few years went by after the stories told in the previous chapter, and one day I got a new idea and decided that I wanted to be my own boss. Having worked in a number of hotels after leaving Scotland, on the Isle of Wight, and in Bournemouth, I thought I would strike out and be my own boss. I decided to go and search for what was on the market, and I put the word out to my friends and agents. I received a call from a friend in Weymouth who told me that there was a hotel that was up for sale on the seafront. I made arrangements to view it, but it would be a joint venture between a friend and myself. The location was perfect; the building had a Georgian terrace with the most spectacular views of the sea, harbour, and hills beyond. We had no hesitation and went ahead to purchase it. It needed a lot of work done and a complete renovation. As we were both builders, we did not see this as a problem. We made an appointment with the bank a few days later. Discussions were held concerning our experience in the hospitality trade. I explained that I had been working in the industry for a number of years. "Well! I'm afraid that's not good enough!" was the response. "Oh, I won't be running it!" I returned and began to explain that my daughter Marina, who has spent a good deal of time working in catering and running pubs. The next day, I went to see Marina, who was then running a letting agency. "How are you, my darling?" I asked in a charming way. "It's a fabulous day, isn't it?" I continued. Marina, of course, knew better and was already suspicious of some sort of tomfoolery going on. "By the way," I said. "I just purchased a hotel in Weymouth." I added with the usual grin on my face, "You're going to be running it." I added. She knew it was going to be a disaster and told me that she wanted nothing to do with my ventures; after all, she knew my history well. I told her I needed her to meet the bank manager and show them her CV, as that was the only way they would finance the deal. She was, of course, adamant and kept refusing while shaking her head in disagreement. Her boss was loitering at the back of the office.

He wore a wig. "Come here, darling," I whispered in her ear that I was going to nick his wig and run out the door. "So I'll count to ten, nine...". I got to five; she turned pink and said, "I'll call you tonight," knowing full well I would have carried out my threat. Marina, of course, ended up calling Anne, saying, "Do you know what he's done?" "Surprise me," came the acid response. Anyway, the purchase went ahead. We started to renovate and opened up. One day, this beautifully dressed lady appeared at the front desk and asked for the owner. I came down and introduced myself. Without wasting any time, she said, "I believe you have a cellar," to which I told her that I did, but it's just being renovated like the rest of the building. She requested that I take her down there so she could have a look around. We went down to the cellar, and for a short while she was looking around and saying, "This is perfect!" She explained that she runs a brothel nearby and wants to expand a little, and my cellar would make a perfect torture chamber for her clients. She began telling me where the various devices would be located. I was just standing there in a state of shock while listening to her. She actually invited me to lunch the next day to discuss things further and the money that would be involved. In the meantime, another offer has been made that was a bit less shocking. I knew I had to make a decision quickly as the Olympics were on and the town was really buzzing. I didn't know the area too well; the last time I was down in Weymouth, I was busy stealing the trousers of the sand sculpture of Rupert the Bear, which my friend Phil spent countless hours perfecting. The offer was about installing massive lights on the ceiling of the cellar along with humidifiers, which would have enabled to create the right atmosphere for certain kinds of plants. I had never run an underground botanic garden before, so I got curious. I came into the reception one morning, and three guests were standing there looking quite upset. "How are you today?" I asked cheerily. "Not good!" they replied with a bitter tone. I would have fainted had their reply been any different.

"Oh, what's the problem?" I asked, which only enabled them to launch a series of moans. "The water isn't coming out of the shower fast enough!" said one of them with his hair still wet. "Oh! I will sort it out straight away." I said as I turned on my heels, remembering that these people had been complaining about everything for the entire week. So out to the back of the kitchen, I went and returned with three bars of soap and placed a bar in each one of their hands. Then I pointed across the promenade to the sea. "Go over there! You won't have any problems; there is plenty of water!" I said while laughing. They obviously protested and told me that they wouldn't accept being spoken to like that. "Piss off then!" I said. The story made the front page of the evening paper, and a reporter called to ask a few questions, including if I regretted it. I told him, "I'd do it again without any hesitation, you should have seen the look on their faces!" They also reported me to the local council, and I was fined £1.200. Small price for such a good laugh. Then there was a serious incident as well, which you will be able to read about in the next appendix. The complaints were consistent, and eventually we had mystery guests stay too in order to investigate. In the end, the bailiffs took mostly everything away, and the place got shut down. So this was the story of me being a hotel owner for a brief period of nine months. On that note, I want to add that it was not only bad complaints, as I have met a lovely lady, who stayed at the hotel multiple times. A quiet and kind lady, she was always by herself, minding her own business. One day I approached her, and we had a conversation, and I asked her what she did. She introduced herself as Vera Kalashnikova, and she told me she was writing a book. Later on, when her book was released, I received a signed copy that included a short message thanking me for my kindness. I have it to this day. On a sunny afternoon, I was watching the bailiffs take all the stuff away, and as I sat there, Phil showed up. He was still complaining about Rupert's stolen trousers. We decided to get a pint, so off we trotted down to the pub.

He was talking in quite a nostalgic way, which I've soon picked up on. He asked me if I remembered the old stories in Fife and our time spent working at Butlins. I said, Of course I did, and asked him if his ribs still hurt after being kicked while scraping around in the rabbit hutch. We laughed a lot, and eventually we got to the story when we went to work in Germany together. The story went like this: Phil was a true legend. I took him to work with me as a carpenter in Germany, and we ended up in Munich on a building site near the football stadium. The building site was a shithole, and it was freezing. Our foreman was a towering German whom I can only describe as Popeye's mate Pluto. He was a big animal. Phil had requested that I teach him some German so that he could pretend to know something about the job. I knew a little German as my wife at the time, Evie, tried to teach me some, but only the naughty and the cursing ones stuck. The German lesson began, and I told Phil to memorise a sentence a day. That will eventually add up, and he will grow his knowledge day by day. The first sentence went like this: "Entschuldigen Sie bitte, kann ich mit Ihrem Pimmel spielen?" The next morning, at 7:30 AM, we arrived at the building site, and the foreman just walked past the entrance. Phil was eager to impress him with his extensive German knowledge, even though he had no clue what it meant. So he went up to this big animal and said, "Entschuldigen Sie bitte, kann ich mit Ihrem Pimmel spielen?" The foreman exploded in fury, cussing at Phil and shouting, "Pervers! Pervers!" We all died laughing. The job came to an abrupt end after that. The next week we were off to find better luck in Amsterdam, Holland, so we got on a train with our tools. A few hours into the trip, we met a group of guys coming back from a trip in India. We got quite friendly, and they invited us to their place in Amsterdam to have a laugh. Phil and I agreed, and we went with them. Unbeknownst to us, they were squatters at the time, staying in an area full of squatters illegally. We spent the whole night with them and had a good time.

We had so much to drink that we ended up passing out when the night came to an end. The next morning, we woke up to an unearthly scene. That day, the bailiffs decided to chase all the squatters out of the area, and they did so while dressed up as Santa Claus. So we were watching about fifty or so Santas breaking windows with hoses and spraying water into houses, chasing people away. The story actually made it to television later on. Phil, of course, remembered this story too, even though it happened all these years ago. We continued to have a few more pints in the pub we were sitting in, and then, as the day came to a close, we both headed home. I made it back to Bournemouth after our little trip down memory lane, and I was busy pottering around in the kitchen while Anne was teaching in the front studio when I heard someone at the front door. Anne answered it unknown to me, and it was Monkey Paul who was told that I was in the kitchen. In, he came. "Okay, I need my money, or I'll tell Anne!" he said in a threatening voice. "Give me a break," I pleaded. "I'm skint!" The threats continued, and out of the corner of my eye, I spotted a little plastic container with gold in it. When Paul first came in, in the corridor, a young lad was fixing the door, and Paul inquired as to who he was working for. "Charlie," was his reply. "Don't work for him; he won't pay you!" The lad didn't know what to make of him. I asked Paul, "Okay, would you accept gold instead?" "What do you mean?" he asked with curiosity. "Oh, no, I can't give you the gold, Anne would go crazy." He had taken the bait. I told him I'd already gone to the pawn broker and cashed some in, explaining that the gold had belonged to her brother, who was a jeweller, and had died. "Let me see it." He took it off the shelf, and I showed it to him. "No, no, I can't give it to you," I said, repeating that Anne would go crazy if I gave it to him. He looked at it and said he'd take it to the jewellers up the road. "No," I said, "take it to Boscombe, they give better prices, that's five miles away. I owe you £80, but that's worth a lot more. Hold onto it until I check the gold price in the Times." "No, no," he said.

The price of gold had gone through the roof. He then promised to bring my change back and was just on his way up the corridor when he turned and showed the young carpenter his pot of gold. "Charlie is okay, really." He said that and left with a smirk on his face. Half an hour went by when there was a bang on the door. Anne opened it. "Where is that bastard?" Paul shouted. "What is it?" Anne asked in a surprised tone. Paul came rushing into the kitchen. Zoe was there. The jeweller told him, after he'd tried to cash his gold in, "Oh yes, that'll look great sprinkled on your Christmas tree!" Well, everyone cried with laughter. Zoe said while laughing, "Paul, how could you fall for that?" He begged me not to tell anyone, and of course, being a good mate, I told everyone. Not all that glitters is gold! The reason he got the name Monkey Paul is because he used to take pictures on the beach with monkeys. Well, one day we decided to go back to his place for a drink in the afternoon, where the monkeys were kept at the rear of the house in the garden. There were four or five of them. We were near the house when smoke was spotted coming from the rear garden. It was a disaster. Somehow, a fire broke out in the cage, and all the monkeys were killed. These were his babies. He broke down. Half an hour went by. He'd had a drink and calmed down a bit, when he asked whether I would like something to eat. I said with an evil grin on my face, "Yes, actually, I'm quite hungry; some monkey on toast would be nice." That set him off again. I'm a heartless bastard. Quite some time has passed since the last story, and there are plenty more that I've left out. This book of mine has spent twenty years in the making, with multiple runs on and off and multiple scriptwriters giving it a go. However, due to my nature and my blood, many times I was the one standing in the way of it on various occasions, and now that it is drawing near to a conclusion, I'm going to try to wrap it up with the last stories. It was a bright, sunny day early in April 2024, and I decided to go out for a walk.

As I was heading back home through the park, I heard somebody playing the blues on an acoustic guitar. I looked around, and I've spotted the source where the music came from. A young fella, perhaps in his late-twenties, was sitting on a bench, playing near the fountain. I could describe him as being rather wan, a bit ill-looking, and very thin. He had large, bright green eyes surrounded by a sleepless complexion, partially covered by his thin, long brown hair. He was dressed in ill-fitting, flower-patterned handmade trousers, a long black cardigan, a shirt with a prism printed on it, and a pencil behind his right ear. I decided to approach him. "Well played, son!" I said, as his slightly lousy blues performance was over. He looked up and thanked me with a wistful smile. I introduced myself and asked him what his name was. "My name is Sacha Rilke," he introduced himself curiously. I went ahead and introduced myself too, and we began talking to each other. After a few exchanges, I told him that I didn't want to interrupt and that I'd be on my way. However, he comforted me by telling me that I'm not disturbing him at all and that he would be happy to have some company. He moved his guitar case off the bench and offered me a seat, which I accepted. We spoke for quite some time, mainly about music, and I asked him if he could sing. He replied with a quiet nod, so I asked him to sing me something. He played and sang a song called "Nobody Home" and when he finished, he looked up at me, perhaps expecting some sort of feedback. I smiled and began to tell him stories about my past as an opera singer, my wife Anne, and the South Coast Opera. He was fascinated, and without speaking a word, he kept listening to everything I had to say. When I finished, he told me that as a child, he was classically trained in music and played the western concert flute, but those times are long gone. He added it with a sigh and stared at the pavement for a little while. As he looked back at me, I asked him cheerfully, "Would you like to meet Anne?" His eyes suddenly lit up, and he gave me a nod and began to pack up his books and his guitar.

After a short walk, we reached my house, and I invited him inside. He was looking around for a while in awe, complimenting the Edwardian styling and the paintings hanging on my walls. I told him to come with me and took him to the studio where Anne teaches her pupils. He was speechless and kept looking around, observing Anne's piano. "Have a go if you like!" I told him, but he respectfully declined, saying he's not worthy. We went to the living room, where Anne was sitting on the sofa, reading. "Look who I brought home!" I said cheerfully and introduced my newfound companion, who was visibly a bit anxious by this time. Anne invited him to take a seat, and we started having a conversation mainly about classical music. I asked him about his background and family. His reply was short and without details. "I'm a bit of a runaway and have been up, down, to and fro while searching for a way to call myself an artist," he said. "Do you want to write a book?" I asked him cheerfully. He thought I was joking and said that he couldn't, as he is neither good nor experienced enough. "Have you ever tried?" I continued questioning. He said, but added that he does write his own lyrics and poetry. "That's good enough!" I said, "Come with me." We went into my working room and told him that I had a book in the making for the last twenty years and that I needed somebody to help.

I began to dig up all the previously handwritten manuscripts and half finished chapters that were lying around in all corners of the room. He began to read them and seemed quite fascinated once again. After a few hours spent in the working room, I convinced him to take on the challenge, and he became my ghost writer. A couple of months passed by, and we were having a little break after finishing the fifth chapter, and I was going through reading the manuscript on my front porch when a white van pulled up by the driveway. Two large men got out and approached me and began to tell me all sorts of things about my roof being close to collapsing and my chimney needing fixing as it is slanted and such.

It was obviously a scam, so I joined in with the game with a usual grin on my face. The man was adamant that my roof would collapse and told me that he runs a roofing business and could give me a discount on fixing it. "Come here, fella!" I told him, and I handed over my book and asked him, "What does that say?" - The Devil's Blood he read it out loud. "That is right! I'm writing it now," I said to him. "I am probably the one who trained your dads in the ways of tomfoolery and scamming." I continued. "It takes one to know one, don't you think?" I've never seen two such large men, with their tails between their legs, get into their van and leave. It certainly is true: "It takes one to know one." Anyway, as I said, there would be so many more stories, probably enough for a second volume, so I'll now begin to come to a conclusion. The reason I always wanted to write this book is to show people that life can be a game and that it truly is "not over 'til the fat lady sings." Growing up in those days was much different with all the poverty, lack of opportunities, etc. But as I always said to myself, necessity creates innovation. In my personal point of view, since everything became so instant and at hand, the necessity simply disappeared. Young people nowadays don't seem to have any humour at all and get upset and personally hurt about the slightest of pranks. All I see everywhere is a strange kind of obsession with their mobile phones and digital equipment. This is something that, in my opinion, needs to be looked into, and raising awareness about it is important for all of us, especially for our children. Anne had a lot of very young pupils during her career as a music teacher, but the interest in recent years has completely disappeared among young people, which is very sad and freightening at the same time. If it weren't for all the arts, be it music, painting, or bookwriting, we would live in a very desolate world. With the words of Friedrich Nietzsche, "We have Art in order not to die of the truth." I would like to conclude with a simple, yet powerful message.

Hold on to your dreams.

Chapter SIX :

"The Soul that Sinneth ...it shall Fly"

Appendix SIX

An original brochure from my brief period of hotel ownership.

"Image source : Charlie McLean's personal collection of memorabilia"

Breakfasts

All Day Breakfast (bacon, sausage, egg, tomato & toast) £2.99
Full English Breakfast (2 sausages, bacon, egg, tomato, mushrooms, beans, 2 toasts) £5.99

Cakes

Scone with strawberry jam & clotted cream £2.60
Toasted tea cake £1.20
Toasted muffins £1.20

Meals

Cheeseburger £2.99
Cod & Chips £4.49
Scampi & Chips £4.99
Homemade Lasagna & Salad £5.99

Kids Meals £2.99

all served with chips & orange juice

Chicken Nuggets
Fish Fingers
Sausages

Jacket Potatoes

all served with butter and salad

Plain £3.50
Bacon & Cheese £3.99
Beans & Cheese £3.99
Tuna & Sweet Corn £4.49
Prawn cocktail £5.49

Sandwiches

Victoria Club Sandwich (chicken & bacon, lettuce & tomato) £4.25
BLT (bacon, lettuce & tomato) £3.50
Hot Local Sausage & Onion £3.50
Tuna Mayonnaise £3.99
Prawn Cocktail £4.99

Drinks

Mineral Water £0.99
Canned Drinks £0.99
Pineapple or Orange Juice £0.95
Tea or Coffee £0.99
Hot Chocolates £1.20
Cappuchino or Latte £1.50

We serve bottled beers & wines

Menu a la Carte "Galloping Gourmet"

"Image source : Charlie McLean's personal collection of memorabilia "

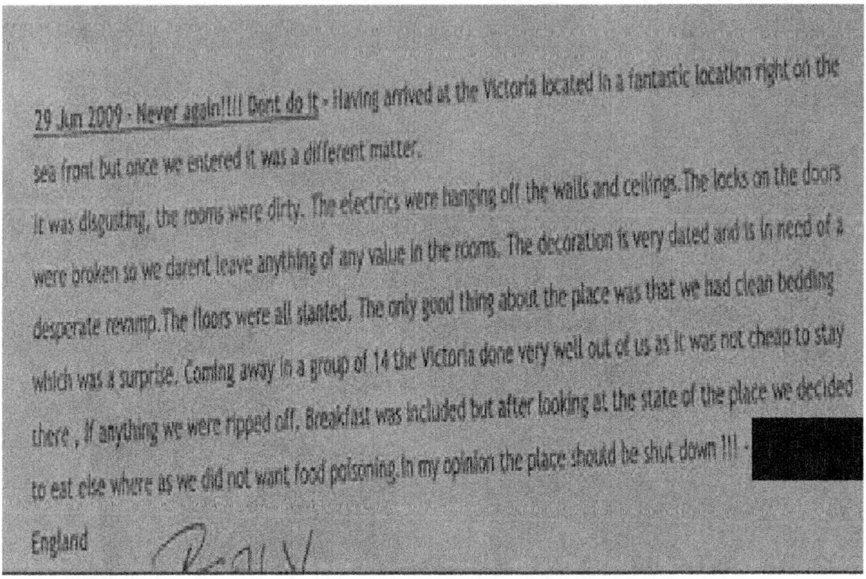

29 Jun 2009 - Never again!!!! Dont do it - Having arrived at the Victoria located in a fantastic location right on the
sea front but once we entered it was a different matter.
it was disgusting, the rooms were dirty. The electrics were hanging off the walls and ceilings.The locks on the doors
were broken so we darent leave anything of any value in the rooms. The decoration is very dated and is in need of a
desperate revamp.The floors were all slanted. The only good thing about the place was that we had clean bedding
which was a surprise. Coming away in a group of 14 the Victoria done very well out of us as it was not cheap to stay
there , if anything we were ripped off. Breakfast was included but after looking at the state of the place we decided
to eat else where as we did not want food poisoning.In my opinion the place should be shut down !!! -
England

Always great to read such kind feedback.

"Image source : Charlie McLean's personal collection of memorabilia (Printed from one of the leading review websites at the time)"

21 Jun 2009 - Please Avoid this Place - Very shabby hotel. Went to Weymouth for the weekend and stayed in the Victoria !! Luckily we were out till the early hours of the morning . The rooms are very basic and in dire need of decorating . The cooked breakfast was ok but not enough to make me want to come back to the Victoria again..............................EVER. You have been warned - ██████

16 Nov 2008 - dirty scrufey hovel - well lets get the best bits over first,the bed was very comfy and the sheets were clean,there was plenty of hot water,and it has a very nice view of the beach now the bad, the whole hotel seems to be decorated in badly done artex and painted magnolia on walls with white ceilings that looked like the icing of a christmas cake.the carpet throughout the whole hotel were stained and filthy dirty.within a few minuites of taking off her trainers my girlfriends white socks were black on the soles from walking on it,after that we kept our shoes on when not in bed. the dust levels under the bed were the worst and a old crisp packet ,hair grip and bottle seal were there as well.the curtains were falling down on one side and i had to rehang them before they could be closed.the very small bathroom was even worse with gatherings of hair under the sink and behind the door,in fact the stains and dirt behind the door made me think perhaps it. had never seen a mop .likewise the shower tray was also stained and dirty.no soap,no bathroom glass,and no shelf in their just a cabinet that was again stained and dirty.no towles upon arrival,when they eventualy came we got 2 very thin hand towels measuring about 15 x 25 inches for the whole of our 2 night stay.we did not have the breakfast in house as standards of cleanliness are so dire that we would not trust what the kitchen was like.and finaly to the story of the chip,when we arrived and were shown to our room my gf saw a chip of the potato variety halfway up the second flight of stairs,it was still there when we went out to eat,it was there when we got back 4 hours later,she said "i bet that still there when we go home on sunday"it was and as far as i know it still maybe. some people should not be allowed to run a hotel,this place is idealy situated opposite the sandist bit of the bay moments from town and all the pubs and clubs, what a waste!

- Liked – views of weymouth beach and bay
- Disliked – dirty carpets,dirty bathroom,dust and decor

██████ - Bristol

5 May 2008 - its a good location but thats all - booked for the may bank holiday weekend 2008

- bed was uncomfortable
- rooms needed a big clean up
- shower wasnt clean or pleasant
- toilet loose on the wall
- floor uneven
- light bulb missing

owner does seem to have been decoraing lately but all badly done

breakfast ok - not very clean in coffee/cereal area - pot of tea not drinkable

owner seemed to have the same clothes on all weekend and didnt always shave

lucky to have parked the car at the back for which he didnt charge us but otherwise parking for most hotels in weymouth seems to be by parking permit which involves a lot of looking for a space.

hotels in a convenient spot and the owner is friendly but inside the hotel leaves a lot to be desired and will not be going there again - ██████

Even more pleased guest's. My personal favourite being the review on the bottom.

"Image source : Charlie McLean's personal collection of memorabilia (Printed from one of the leading review websites at the time)"

Extracts from Website www.█████.co.uk for The Victoria Hotel 56-57 The Esplanade Weymouth

(copied and pasted including grammatical errors)

__26 Aug 2009 - Really Friendly Hotel, Lovely Owners, Excellent Location And Service__ - My mom and I have just come back from this hotel today, we have been there three times and we are already planning our next visit there. The owner and his wife are lovely people and offer an excellent service. They are very kind and give an excellent service, hotel is in a fantastic location, we would not stay at any other hotel in Weymouth, excellent value for money and excellent service. - █████ west midlands

__9 Aug 2009 - Excellent customer service, good rooms, fantastic views and at a great price__ - My boy friend and I stayed at The Victoria Hotel for a week in the beginning of August 2009 and we enjoyed our stay. The service was fantastic, they were friendly, kind, very polite and made our stay enjoyable by making us feel very welcome. The room we stayed in was clean, tidy, adequate size, had a lovely shower, comfy bed and a fantastic view of Weymouth.

The breakfast was fantastic, could not have asked for any more.

The location being at the sea front was great and ideal, the hotel is by the main shops and pubs. It was a bit noisy at the weekend, because the hotel is very close to bars and a club so a family with young children may not be happy with the location but people who are looking for a night out drinking it is a perfect location.

The parking was not very good, there was not enough space but the staff did there best to help with the problem and were very considerate.

For the price we paid for our room for a week it was very good value for money and I would stay there again. Best bits were the value for money, the friendly service and waking up to those fantastic views. Worst bit was probably the noise from the club. - █████ England

__29 Jul 2009 - Friendly cheap hotel ideal for hen/stag parties__ - I have just returned from a hen weekend with a large group of 24 staying at the Victoria, after reading the reviews I was a little concerned before our arrival but for our needs the Victoria was perfect. Ali the owner was very pleasant, helpful and accomodating, the water was hot, sheets clean and was in ideal location with most rooms having a beautiful view over the beach and nearest nightclub a few doors up- ideal for us as we were there to party. We were apprehensive about the breakfast but needn't have been it was delicious! Don't think I'd return with my family as in very noisy location but for cheap, friendly accomodation you couldn't go wrong - █████ Bristol

After all it wasn't only doom and gloom

"Image source : Charlie McLean's personal collection of memorabilia (Printed from one of the leading review websites at the time)"

STAB HORROR

KNIFE ATTACK: Police are hunting a knifeman who stabbed a guest near the Victoria Hotel on Weymouth seafront. Inset: Dave Price of the Weymouth Hoteliers Association

Police launch manhunt after guest is knifed near town hotel

The local paper advertising my hotel

"Image source : Charlie McLean's personal collection of memorabilia"

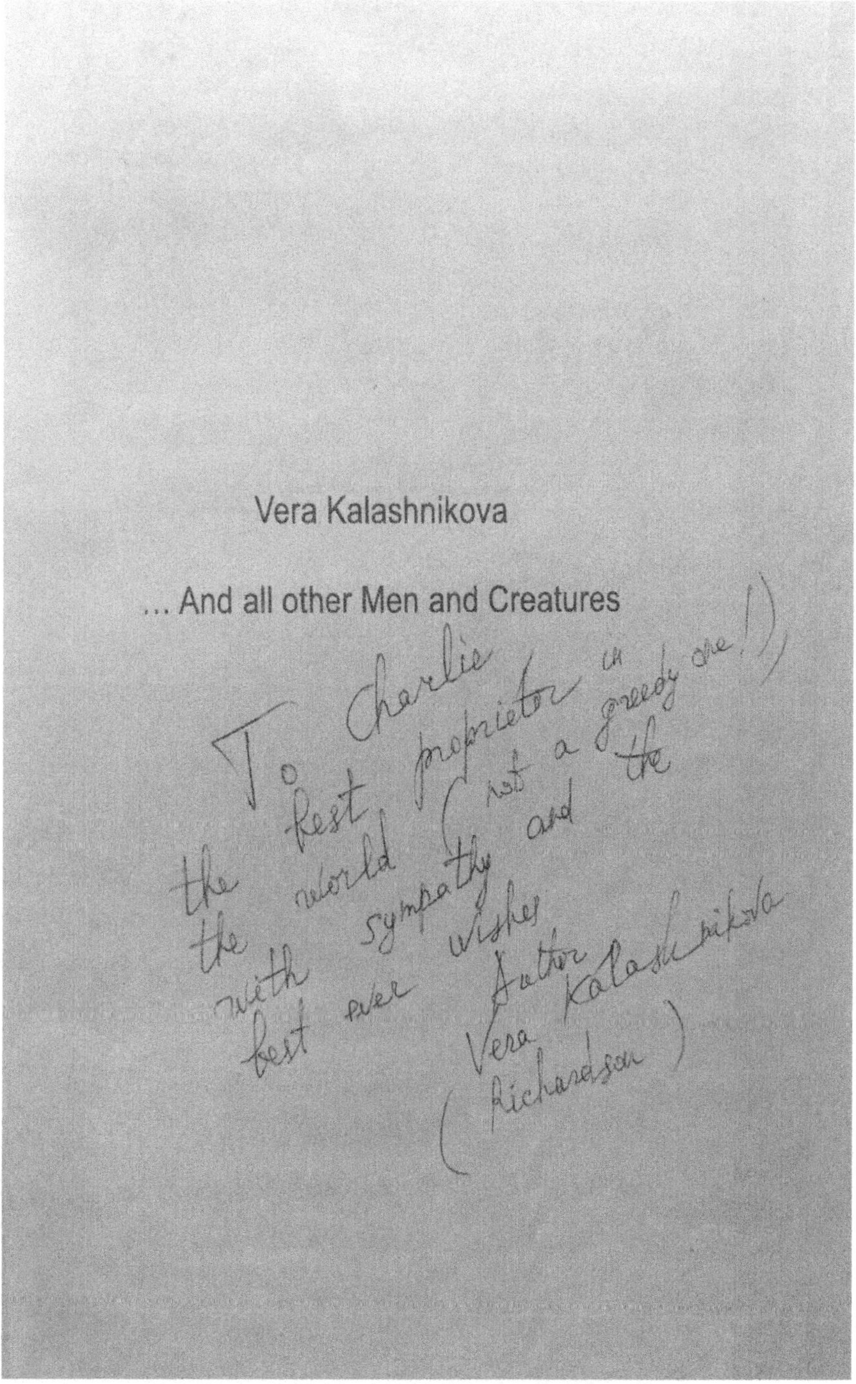
Vera Kalashnikova

... And all other Men and Creatures

To Charlie
the best proprietor in
the world (not a greedy one!)
with sympathy and the
best ever wishes
Author
Vera Kalashnikova
(Richardson)

A truly wonderful book! I highly recommend reading it.

Thank you Vera Kalashnikova!

Skywalker Ranch

"Image source : Charlie McLean's personal collection of memorabilia"

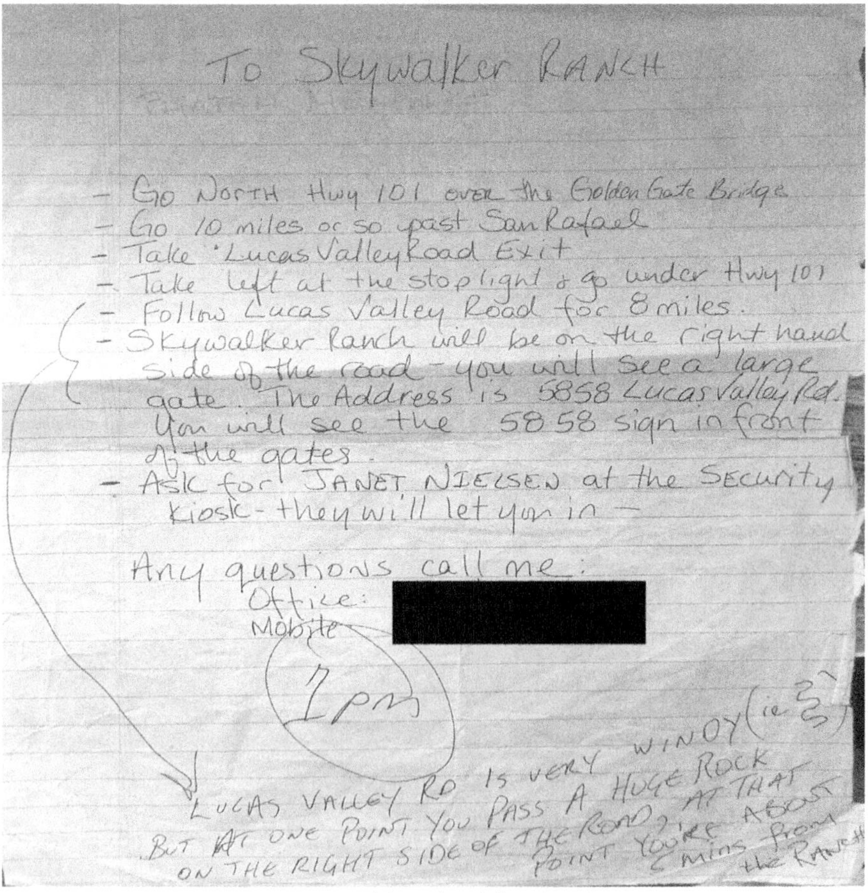

TO Skywalker RANCH

- GO NORTH Hwy 101 over the Golden Gate Bridge
- Go 10 miles or so past San Rafael
- Take 'Lucas Valley Road Exit
- Take left at the stop light & go under Hwy 101
- Follow Lucas Valley Road for 8 miles.
- Skywalker Ranch will be on the right hand side of the road - you will see a large gate. The Address is 5858 Lucas Valley Rd. You will see the 5858 sign in front of the gates.
- Ask for JANET NIELSEN at the Security kiosk - they will let you in -

Any questions call me:
Office:
Mobile

7pm

LUCAS VALLEY RD IS VERY WINDY (ie ~~) BUT AT ONE POINT YOU PASS A HUGE ROCK ON THE RIGHT SIDE OF THE ROAD, AT THAT POINT YOU'RE ABOUT 5 mins from the RANCH

... and how to get there!

"Image source : Charlie McLean's personal collection of memorabilia"

NEWS (TELEVISION)

THE BRITISH BROADCASTING CORPORATION

Head Office: BROADCASTING HOUSE, LONDON, W.1

Broadcasting House, 21-25, Whiteladies Road, Bristol, 8.

TELEPHONE AND TELEGRAMS: BRISTOL 33211

27th January, 1967.

Our Reference: 14010/FS/CMH

DEAR Sir,

With reference to our invitation to you to prepare and deliver a news report in our television programmes we offer you an engagement on the terms and conditions shown below and overleaf. If you accept, kindly sign and return the attached confirmation sheet, or reply otherwise, as soon as possible. (See condition 1 overleaf).

Title: 'SOUTH TODAY' 164/3/6/9359 - Modelled mini-kilt during interview.

Region of origin: West.

Date of Recording (or filming): -

Place: Southampton.

Date of First Broadcast: 25th January, 1967.

Time of First Broadcast: 5.58 - 6.17 p.m.

Fee: £4 4s. 0d. + return rail fare Bournemouth/Southampton. (Please indicate).

Letters addressed to speakers c/o the BBC will be forwarded, but for statistical purposes the letters may be opened before being forwarded unless we are notified of any objection. Letters marked "Personal" are forwarded unopened. If you should receive notice of any claim for defamation in respect of the report(s) you are asked to notify the Corporation before taking any steps to deal with the claim.

Yours faithfully,

THE BRITISH BROADCASTING CORPORATION

West Regional Programme Executive

C. McLean, Esq.,
22 Lorne Park Road,
Bournemouth,
Hants.

P/26 11 65 AEB

As I said before: I could tell many more stories.

Perhaps I will in Volume 2.

"Image source : Charlie McLean's personal collection of memorabilia"

CHARLIE McLEAN

TUNE HOUSE OF THE RISING SUN WORDS BY F WILSON

THERE WAS A MAN DOWN BOURNEMOUTH WAY LISTEN CLOSE I'LL
TELL HIS NAME
BUT FIRST I'LL TELL YOU OF THIS LAD AND FROM
THE TOWN HE CAME
OF BROTHERS THREE HE WAS THE CLOWN THE OTHER
TWO WERE SANE
FROM COWDENBEATH THESE LADS DID COME THEIR NAME
IT WAS McLEAN

HE PLUGGED THE SCHOOL HE ROBBED THE PRIEST AND DRANK
HIS HOLY WATTER
BUT WHEN CONFRONTED BY THE LAW THEY COULD'NT STAND
HIS PATTER
SO DOWN TO BOURNEMOUTH HE DID RUN TO FIND A LIFE
OF CLOVER
AND WHEN HE SAW THE BIRDS DOWN HERE HE KNEW HIS
SEARCH WAS OVER

TO PULL THESE GIRLS WAS SIMPLE STUFF OUR HERO WAS
A CHANCER
BUT THEY LOVED MONEY SO HE THOUGHT I'LL BE A
LANDSCAPE GARDENER
WHEN BUILDING WALLS AND PLANTIN TREES HIS ONLY
TOOL A SPOON
BUT LIKE THE WALLS OF JERICHO THE MOST OF THEM
FELL DOON

WITH A MALLET AND A BOW SAW BLADE HE THOUGHT HE'D
BE A CHIPPIE
BUT THE PRICE OF PENCILS WENT SKYHIGH SO HE ENDED
UP A HIPPIE
HIS BROTHERS JAMES AND WULLIE MADE FORTUNES AT
THESE GAMES
BUT AS I TOLD YOU EARLIER THE PAIR OF THEM
WERE SANE

OUR HERO HE GOT SICK OF THIS CADGIN ROUND ALL
THE BARS
A VISION TO HIM ONE NIGHT CAME I THINK I'LL SELL
SOME CARS
NOW LISTEN ALL YOU CHILDREN DONT DO WHAT OUR
MAN DONE
SPEND YOUR LIFE IN TOTAL MISERY YOU NEVER
SEE THE SUN

SO IF YOU COME TO BOURNEMOUTH FOR A HOLIDAY
BY THE SEA
DONT BUY A CAR FROM ANYONE WHO SINGS DOON
ON ONE KNEE
SO FATHERS WATCH YOUR DAUGHTERS AND SAVE YOURSELF
SOME PAIN
YER MAN IS ON THE LOOSE AGAIN WATCH OUT FOR
CHARLIE McLEAN.

On a finishing note a poem written about ...
By a great friend who unfortunately passed away.
Thank you for reading my book "The Devil's Blood"

"Image source : Charlie McLean's personal collection of memorabilia"

On this last page of the Devil's Blood I would like to take the opportunity to express how thankful I am for all the help, encouragement, and inspiration that I have received from my family, friends, and all the people close to me.
Without them it would have never been possible to complete this 20 year dream of mine.

Special Thanks and gratitude to:

Anne T. for being most encouraging and supportive during the working hours and providing her invaluable artistic insight to the creation of the cover art.

Adam Sacha Soveges my co-author for his countless hours of work as a ghost-writer, editor, proofreader, and archivist. He's been a good friend and great support for this book as he worked with manuscripts that in many times were lost to time, and all the conversations that enabled him to write my stories.

All the previous writers whom tried to make a comprehensive memoir out of my constant tomfoolery.

Thank You!
-Mr. Charlie McLean

As a last tomfoolery, I hereby challenge you! The reader! To take my long time honor and title of being the self-proclaimed King of the Jungle Call!
We are accepting recording's of your own version of the famous call to our e-mail address (charlie.mclean941@gmail.com) which we will assess and reply to. After enough material arrived a winner will be announced and upon success I will pass my self-proclaimed title on!

May the best call win!

Printed in Dunstable, United Kingdom

66911995R00087